brew like a MONK

Culture and Craftsmanship in the Belgian Tradition

Trappist, Abbey, and Strong Belgian Ales and How to Brew Them

Stan Hieronymus

With foreword by
Tim Webb

brewers
publications

A Division of the
Brewers Association
Boulder, Colorado

Brewers Publications
A Division of the Brewers Association
PO Box 1679, Boulder, Colorado 80306-1679
www.beertown.org

Printed in the United States of America.

10 9 8 7 6 5 4 3

ISBN-13: 9780937381878
ISBN-10: 0-937-381-87-X

Library of Congress Cataloging-in-Publication Data

Hieronymus, Stan.
  Brew like a monk : Trappist, abbey, and strong Belgian ales
and how to brew them / Stan Hieronymus.
     p. cm.
  ISBN 0-937381-87-X
  1. Beer. 2. Brewers--Religious life--Belgium--History. 3.
Brewers--Religious life--United States--History. 4.
Trappists--Spiritual life. 5. Cookery (Beer) I. Title.

  TP577.H546 2005
  663'.42'088255125--dc22

                   2005020617

Publisher: Ray Daniels
Technical Editor: Randy Mosher
Copy Editor: Daria Labinsky
Index: Daria Labinsky
Production & Design Management: Stephanie Johnson
Cover and Interior Design: Julie Lawrason
Cover Illustration: Alicia Buelow
Cover Photo, "Brother Lode Orval": Owen Franken
Photos: Stan Hieronymus

To Saint Benedict and all the monastery brewers he inspired.

table of
Contents

PART III—BREWING YOUR OWN

Acknowledgements

My long list of people to thank begins with those on the ground in Belgium: Derek Walsh, Yvan De Baets, and Joris Pattyn—their guidance kept me from getting hopelessly lost. Derek provided most of the important data for tables that allow us to "strip search" (his words) the Trappist beers, as well as many images. I also would have been lost without Tim Webb's *Good Beer Guide to Belgium & Holland* (CAMRA, 2002) and thank him for the Foreword as well. Several importers helped me work with Belgian brewers but especially Dan Shelton and Craig Hartinger, without whose help the following pages would be short essential information. No book was more valuable than Jef van den Steen's *Les Trappistes: Les Abbayes et Leurs Bières* (Editions Racine, 2003), which offers details about Trappist brewing history and current practices that nobody else has reported, as well as spectacular photos.

Everybody who writes about beer owes a serious debt to Michael Jackson, more serious still when it comes to the beers of Belgium. By writing about them nearly thirty years ago—

that's when Schlitz was a top-selling beer in America—he provided a history we wouldn't otherwise enjoy. I also owe triple thanks to Ray Daniels, because he suggested I write this book, then kept me on track, and because *Designing Great Beers* (Brewers Publications, 1996) provided clues about how to organize it. Along those lines, thanks to Gordon Strong for two presentations aimed at homebrewers, one titled "Designing Great Dubbels, Everything You Wanted to Know About Belgians But Were Afraid to Ask Ray," that helped me get my bearings when it came to approaching this family of beers.

Brock Wagner, founder of Saint Arnold Brewing Company in Houston, Texas, has said, "I've come to realize I may own the stock, but it's not my brewery. It belongs to everybody who drinks Saint Arnold beer." I should write the same of this book. I assembled it, but the book belongs to hundreds of commercial and amateur brewers who provided the information you'll find here. I thank them and apologize in advance to those whose names don't get listed. I raise a glass to every brewer quoted in this book and every one who took the time to contribute.

Basically, I thank everyone who went out of their way to keep me from looking stupid. For instance, Siebel Institute of Technology and World Brewing Academy put both volumes of Jean De Clerck's essential *A Textbook of Brewing* (Chapman & Hall, 1957) in the mail when I needed them, and Anheuser-Busch sent a book from its corporate library. Many brewers, even those inside monastery walls, took the time to exchange multiple e-mails and clarify important details.

Along those lines, particular thanks go to Randy Mosher, not just for books I consulted often when writing this one, but for material I otherwise would not have found and for being the last line of defense when it came to technical matters.

I reserve the most special thanks for my wife, Daria, the best copy editor a wayward beer writer could want, a perfect beer traveling companion, and the woman who encourages me to pursue sometimes frivolous endeavors. Also thanks to our children, Sierra and Ryan, for being generally inspiring.

Foreword
by Tim Webb

I used to live in an area of south-west England called the South Hams. The area is east of Plymouth, where the Pilgrim Fathers stocked up the Mayflower on its journey from Holland to the New World. It is a place of ancient villages and holiday homes, snuck between the moorland of Sherlock Holmes' *Hound of the Baskervilles* and the coastal creeks where Sir Francis Drake lay in wait for the Spanish Armada.

When I moved there my first task, obviously, was to locate the best of the local pubs. Finding them was easy enough—it is an area blessed with the best of the breed—but remembering which was which was more difficult. The reason was that so many were called by the same name, the Church House Inn. I recall there were ten, unrelated in business.

It was not until a decade later, when researching the second edition of the *Good Beer Guide to Belgium*, that I realized what these venerable places had in common. They had all been hostelries that had graced the front gates of long-dead abbeys, priories, and monasteries.

I had learned of such places at junior school, from the redoubtable Colonel Gethin. A crusty old survivor of the war in Mesopotamia in 1916, the Sixties saw Gethin teaching History and General Knowledge in the British Midlands. His style was to replace the curriculum with a boiled-down version of his own experiences of life. Condemned to be ignorant of official history, we were instead inspired to understand what makes the world as it is.

The Colonel's take on Christianity was that it was a great force, for good and evil. Taking monasteries as the best example of this, he told us they were places of scholarship and learning, in much the same way as modern universities. Yet, equally, they were despised as hotbeds of political intrigue and influence, usually of a most unchristian variety.

Yet they got away with their reputations intact, in this version of history at any rate, "because they provided good lodgings!" Just as the populace forgave Mussolini's fascistic barbarism because he made the trains run on time.

People of taste and influence have always been smart travelers. In the centuries before *Lonely Planet*, well-informed travellers knew that the best lodgings were at the inns run by abbeys. Plain but clean rooms, fellowship, bread, cheese, fresh produce, and, of course, ale, a speciality of monks throughout the centuries.

The fact that the tradition of brewing abbeys survives until the twenty-first Christian century is a testament to its association with high quality. That its survival is currently limited to the kingdom of Belgium and to the Cistercian Order of the Strict Observance, or Trappists, is more a quirk of history.

Monastic brewing is known to have existed as far back as the sixth century. Saint Benedict, on whose rules the whole monastic system is based, encouraged abbeys to contribute to their local community. On public health grounds alone, brewing beer was a noble act. In times of water-borne epidemics, the boiling of beer during brewing made it a far healthier option than the town's water supply.

Brewing survived in abbeys beyond Belgium until relatively recently.

In France the abbeys at Mont des Cats in French Flanders, Sept Fons in the northern Auvergne, Chambarand in the Rhône Alps, and Oelenberg in Alsace were still brewing in the first years of the twentieth century.

The only Trappist abbey in Germany, at Mariawald near Aachen in the Eiffel region next to the Belgian border, was still selling *Mariawalder Klosterbräu* in 1956, though whether they still brewed it is unclear. At Tegelen abbey in the Netherlands, brewing continued on a commercial scale until 1950.

Monks at the abbey of Notre-Dame des Mokoto, a hundred miles north of Goma in the Democratic Republic of Congo, brewed for their personal consumption until 1996, when it was destroyed in the region's civil war.

Belgium's association with modern monastic brewing owes a lot to the timing of its emergence as a nation. Belgium was born in 1830 as an independent democratic monarchy. It enjoyed religious freedom, although its population was mainly Catholic.

Neighboring France had been a republic for just over forty years. Its first great leader, Napoleon Bonaparte, had sacked the monasteries. Only fifteen years after his final defeat at the Battle of Waterloo, just south of the Belgian capital, Brussels, it became clear that the new kingdom would be tolerant of monks.

The first Belgian Trappist abbey to revive brewing was Westmalle in 1836. Then came Westvleteren in 1839 and Chimay in 1850. In 1881, near Tilburg in the Netherlands, the abbey at Schaapskooi started brewing. Saint-Rémy at Rochefort started up in 1892. At Orval abbey, which reopened in 1926, the brewery that opened in 1931 was an integral part of the business plan for repaying the cost of reconstruction.

In 1998 the brewing world was surprised and delighted at the news that a seventh abbey brewery was to open at Achel, bang on the Dutch border in northern Belgium. A year later, amidst much sadness, Schaapskooi abbey lost its monastic accreditation.

Romancers and people who design coasters love the idea of monks brewing beer. Of course, it is not really done that way any more. All the brewing abbeys, except Westvleteren, are under the auspices of a lay brewing director and have been for decades.

The designation of a beer as "Trappist" is defined neither by the workforce that makes it nor the style in which it is brewed. It is a legal definition.

In 1962 the Belgian government tried to limit the use of the term Trappist by law to beers brewed within a monastery. However, this law was hard to implement in practice, so in 1992 the term "Authentic Trappist Product" became in effect a trademark.

The brand is bestowed with the permission of the Vatican on cheeses, breads, liqueurs, perfumes, soaps, and many other goods, as well as beers. To qualify for acceptance, a product must be made within the walls of a Trappist abbey, under the supervision of the monastery community, and the largest part of the profit from its sale must be spent on social work.

Monks are not expected to control a monastery brewery by deciding when to turn the kettle down or stop emptying the grain silo into the mash. They control it by determining the brewery's operational policies and strategic approach.

Although their motivation for trying to turn a profit is entirely different, the determination of these breweries to be commercially successful is exactly the same as for a limited company. Indeed, the dilemma that afflicts monastic brewing at the beginning of the twenty-first century has its origins here.

The companies that run the Westmalle and Chimay breweries make no bones about the fact that they are commercial concerns that seek to be successful in the international beer market. And as everywhere else, the companies seek to drive costs down while keeping profits high.

Westmalle has always been open about using candi sugar in brewing. It has done this for so many years that it is an integral part of the beers. Westvleteren also uses sugar. Rochefort uses sugar and wheat starch, and Orval, straight sugar. Chimay deploys starch, with proportions as high as 34% quoted by some sources, although 29% is probably closer the mark. Their starch is derived from wheat.

Chimay claims to have replaced hops with tinned hop extract, the consistency of industrial jam, thirty years ago. In common with most other Belgian brewers, and in sharp contrast to other craftbrewing cultures, the use of whole hops in monastic beers is rare. This may account for why Belgium is not famed for its great hop recipes.

They have got away with these brewing shortcuts over the years by employing careful and time-consuming fermentation. Some have also done clever things with conditioning, such as Orval's twin tricks of dry-hopping the lagering tanks and adding *Brettanomyces* for bottle-conditioning.

Unfortunately, in the permanent, and I for one think misguided, quest to keep down production costs, the recent falls in the quality of the fermented beers are now revealing the effects of flawed recipes rather more than was previously the case.

At Rochefort the taste impact of the beers has diminished a little, through reduction in lagering time and, I suspect, by rather too enthusiastic filtration. In Chimay and Westmalle beers one finds the acrid backtastes of fast fermentation, set against a backdrop of *svelte* character. *Orval* remains a classic brew but is less extreme in its statements and is the smaller for that.

The abbeys' dilemma here strikes me as simple. To maximise income at a time when demand outstrips supply, one has either to make more beer or charge more for it, or both.

Ratebeer.com (*www.ratebeer.com*) users recently voted *Westvleteren Abt* (*12*) as the best beer in the world. At an alcohol content of 10.3% by volume, it is on a par with many wines, though with an intensity more associated with a fortified Shiraz than a flimsy Moselle. Yet at the café outside the gates of Sint-Sixtus abbey near Westvleteren, the equivalent of a wine bottle's worth costs about $5.95. And that is retail.

Does that sound like the price of the best in the world to you?

Does it really make sense for the family of beers that has the most legitimate claim to aspire to higher values, to want to cut it with the world's tinned super-strength lagers in the student and bums market? Would it not be more worthy for monastic beers to adopt a more contemplative style. To become Slow Beer, in the manner of Slow Food. Fine ingredients honed to perfection in the time that God intended for such processes?

In a head-to-head tasting of Belgian-style abbey beers made by American microbrewers, in Arlington, Virginia, in early 2005, I was shocked to find that the American imitations were knocking the socks off certain freshly imported "real" Trappist ales.

I should not have been. After all, the Belgians have been imitating them for years, and some the pretenders, such as *St. Bernardus, Kapittel, Witkap, Dupont,* and *St Feuillien,* are way better than most of the originals.

So if you want to brew like a monk, what should you do? Not imitate current practice, that is for sure.

Perhaps the best advice would be to brew with good intentions.

Tim Webb
Editor
The Good Beer Guide to Belgium
www.booksaboutbeer.com

Introduction

THE TRAPPIST BRAND

You could say that Gumer Santos has a homebrewer's dream job. As a chemical engineering student, Santos would study in the quiet of the Abbey Notre-Dame de Saint-Rémy near Rochefort. "We were many students. We came to the abbey to study," Santos said. "And I kept a good relationship with the monks here."

One day the father abbot asked Santos if he would like to work in the brewery at Rochefort, one of six Trappist breweries in the world. The monks would send him to the Catholic University of Leuven to become a brewing engineer. "I asked him if he knew I produced beer at home with a friend," Santos said. "We made classic blonde beer."

Santos spends most of his working time in the laboratory or otherwise focusing on process. He reports to Vital Streignard, who is director of production. Streignard must account to Brother Pierre, one of six monks who work in the brewing operation and the one ultimately responsible for the quality of the beer.

Authentic Trappist Product

Trappist monks and Trappistine nuns belong to the Cistercian Order of the Strict Observance, with about a hundred houses of monks and seventy of nuns worldwide. Trappists take their name from a reform movement that started in the seventeenth century at a French monastery, La Trappe.

At the beginning of 2005, eight Trappist abbeys—six Belgian, one Dutch (Tegelen), and one German (Mariawald)—belonged to the International Trappist Association, offering their products under the hexagonal logo of "Authentic Trappist Product." Only the six in Belgium brew beer. They are:

- Saint Benedictusabdij de Acheles Kluis. Achel beers.
- Abbaye Notre-Dame de Scourmont. Chimay beers.
- Abbaye Notre-Dame de Saint-Rémy. Rochefort beers.
- Abbaye Notre-Dame d'Orval. Orval beers.
- Abdij der Trappisten van Westmalle. Westmalle beers.
- De Sint-Sixtusabdij van Westvleteren. Westvleteren beers.

To use the name and the logo on any merchandise, including beer, the rules of the International Trappist Association must be observed:

- The product must be made within the walls of a Trappist abbey.
- The product must be made by or under the supervision of the monastery community.
- The largest part of the profit must be spent on social work.

"Abbey beers" are something different. They may or may not be "certified." More on them in Chapter 4.

One day early in 2005, a customer returned half a case of *Rochefort 6* to the brewery. He even brought a short video, showing himself pouring the beer and the head collapsing almost immediately. He passed along friends' claims the beer didn't taste right. Santos watched the video a second time, then hauled out his brewing log. Because all Belgian beers must carry a "best before" date, he knew just the day the beer had been brewed and bottled.

Santos opened a bottle from what remained in the case. This one poured a bit fizzy ("We call that singing," he said), but the head lingered properly. The sample tasted perfect, even as the beer warmed. Santos looked in his log. "Nothing different that day. It could have been at the beginning or end of the bottling (run)," he said, trying to explain why some bottles would have been off, and others fine. Rochefort bottle-conditions its beers with fresh yeast and sugar. Because the brewery mixes beer, yeast, and sugar in a bottling tank, every bottle may not

Gumer Santos used to study at Rochefort. Now he monitors the quality of its beer.

get the exact same dose. He explained that in the future a stamp on the Rochefort labels would include not only a date but also a time, and he would be able to tell where in the run a bottle was filled.

"I didn't go to school to come up with a revolution. Study should be a plus for the quality of the beer," Santos said. "We use the same recipe as in the 1950s. This is the big rule of all the Trappist breweries. You don't change anything. (I) understand chemically and biologically what happens. It's not always possible to control exactly what happens, and in the case of a problem we need to be able to react."

With such attention to detail, Trappists developed a classic brand, if not a singular beer style. In fact, the hexagonal "Authentic Trappist Product" logo is literally branded into the wooden crates from Westvleteren. Sure, the monastic storyline helped, but they finally set themselves apart in the marketplace based on quality. The beers didn't taste better because they were produced according to an 800-year-old recipe handed down from monk to monk, but because brewers, sometimes monks and sometimes not, worked hard to make them better.

The defenders of the Trappist brand include brewing engineers such as Santos and monks such as Brother Joris at the Abbey of Saint Sixtus at Westvleteren, who keeps busy as monastery librarian as well as brewery supervisor. "I am just trying to keep the business going," Brother Joris said, modestly. A little later, he cocked an eyebrow and smiled as he surveyed the cellar where beer was lagering. "It is a good day," he said. "There isn't any beer dripping from the tanks."

Although Trappists may argue that their policy prohibits modifying recipes, their beers reflect changes in brewing practices and availability of ingredients. For instance, Chimay, Rochefort, and Orval converted primary fermentation to cylindro-conical tanks. The changes weren't made without forethought. In the case of Orval, the brewery staff spent five years tasting and blending beer that came from one conical before putting five more on line in 2004. Rochefort decided to fill its fermenters only halfway to the top, keeping more horizontal dimensions. "In all the books, you can read that cylinders change the taste, but this way these don't," Santos said. "Everything we can measure is the same."

But flavor memories can be fleeting. Famed beer writer Michael Jackson has written about this on more than one occasion, commenting a few years ago on how Chimay sold its beer in far-flung parts of the world. "In search of yet-wider sales, will these beers dumb down?" he asked. "I hope not, though I feel that Chimay has lost some character. If they do, they will be replaced by others in the connoisseurs' affections."

In the Foreword for this book, Tim Webb also warns of the danger of blindly worshiping these beers simply because monasteries produce them. Westvleteren, the least commercial of the Trappist breweries, operates with commercial intent; the profits just happen to go to running the abbey and for various charities. The Trappists take pride that equipment will be modernized in a timely fashion, in their laboratories, and in the fact they oversee production rather than contracting it out to equally commercial breweries that allocate their profits differently. Monks can quantify such things, but measuring the quality of their beer presents a different challenge, because most monks drink little, if at all.

As the twenty-first century began, Rochefort made its conversion to cylindro-conical tanks, installed a second centrifuge (also known as a polishing machine) to remove residual trub after secondary fermentation, and had to change malt suppliers

The author with Brother Antoine, who was in charge of brewing at Rochefort for twenty-one years, and brewing engineer Gumer Santos. Photo courtesy of Derek Walsh.

when Interbrew closed the DeWolf-Cosyns malting facility. Customers noticed that the beer tasted different while Rochefort was making brewing adjustments.

"Some people will say it is better now, some will say that it's worse, but you cannot say it has not changed," said Yvan De Baets, a Belgian native who wrote the chapter on the history of *saison* in *Farmhouse Ales* (Brewers Publications, 2004).

Although Brother Pierre remains more involved than monks at almost any other Trappist brewery, it was reassuring that Brother Antoine—the monk in charge from 1976 to 1997—would also show up in the brewery almost daily. "When I started here (in 2000), he was everywhere," Santos said. "You'd see him at the kettles, then you'd go to the bottling room and he'd be there." Brother Antoine is slighter of build now than in the pictures in Jackson's *The Great Beers of Belgium* (Running Press, 1998) and spends less time in the brewery. Yet on the day I visited he stopped by the brewery with a batch of flowers. He spun a story about a mug from his collection of hundreds of drinking vessels that sit on shelves just outside the bottling room. When he spoke of beer, his eyes came to life, and he tilted his head a bit to the side with a look of pure mischievousness.

Philippe Van Assche, general manager at Westmalle, often is asked why the monks at Westmalle started brewing, or why they decided to take a more commercial turn in 1930 and expand the brewery. He doesn't think that is the interesting question. "You should ask why they should continue to have the brewery," he said. "They would have had many opportunities to sell or license the name, to sell the recipes.

"They look at the breweries on the outside world," he said, pausing and realizing he didn't need to finish that thought.

"The monks' values are present in the way this brewery is run. Production is stable. This is an abbey with a brewery, not the other way around. It is in harmony with the environment. They want to keep the quality of the beer."

Can they? I talked with an enthusiast in Belgium who made a particularly good point. "Monks are not beer geeks," he said. "They are not the ones who will protect the (Trappist) beers." Perhaps not by themselves, but it would be a mistake to think they don't pay attention to what is happening in the outside world or in their own breweries.

"To me, what the monks are saying is very wise," Santos said. "They will say, 'A yeast, to make a good wort, has to be well. If you take care of the yeast, it will give you back a present with good flavor.' The monk will take his finger and dip it in the yeast. He will say, 'Ah, good yeast.' It should remain like that. It is good to take measurements, but don't forget the other aspects."

ABOUT THE BOOK

Could you brew like a monk? Should you? Would you?

In an interview a few years ago, Brother Pierre of Rochefort indicated you certainly could. He said:

"Every brewer with some experience is able to copy our beers perfectly. After the bottling, the yeast cells still keep living for about six months. Anyone wanting our yeast can remove it from the bottom and cultivate it. We use the same culture for the main and second fermentation. Even the malts and hops we use are no secret. Anyone who is determined ... can do so easily. Some brewers do not want to reveal the spices they use for brewing. Well, we only use a dash of coriander."

He does allow it might not be quite that simple. "You know, if there were a secret, it is to be found in our attitude towards life, in our relation with God and with nature. We believe that everything growing on the field or in nature—and what you brew out of it—is not merchandise but a gift. That is no laughing matter. We make our beers as natural as possible without too much profit seeking. The Trappists are not dealing with compromises regarding price or quality."[1]

So should you?

For many commercial brewers, the challenge presents good enough reason. "When we finally brewed it, we were interested in doing it as a fun thing and as an academic exercise as brewers," said North Coast Brewing Company brewmaster Mark Ruedrich, talking about *PranQster.* The beer turned into a profitable regular for the California brewery, and the market for such beers continues to grow. For instance, at Victory Brewing Company in Pennsylvania, *Golden Monkey* (a *tripel*) became the brewery's second-best-selling beer, and *The Reverend* (a *quadrupel*) outsells every other beer Avery Brewing Company in Colorado packages in 22-ounce bottles.

For amateur brewers, dealing with the challenge may be reward enough. Is there anything comparable to the commercial profit some microbrewers enjoy? I don't brew to save money, but given that the cheapest 330ml bottle of Trappist beer sells for nearly $4 in New Mexico, it is easy to justify the extra time and expense involved in brewing these beers.

---

[1] Bob Magerman, "Trappist Beer From Rochefort," *Bier Passion* 11 (April/May 2001): 41.

How would you? Will this book tell you?

Understand that I had spent at least a few years suggesting to Ray Daniels that he write *Designing Great Belgian Beers*. This isn't that book—it became apparent early on that it would take more than one book (which is why this is the third in a series) to chronicle beers inspired by Belgian brewers. I particularly like that *Designing Great Beers* laid out how brewers historical and current, commercial and amateur, brew various styles, then left it up to you to decide who you want to "brew like." Brewing should always be about choices, but never more so than when brewing in the spirit of Belgium.

Chimay Recipe

In *Brewing Beers Like Those You Buy* (G.W. Kent, 1978), the late Dave Line offered a recipe for what he simply called Chimay. The specifications indicate he targeted *Chimay Red*. The recipe (reprinted as it appeared in the book) reflects what ingredients were available to homebrewers in 1978, and the process they would have employed.

Recipe for 3 gallons

Original Gravity 1.075

6.5 lbs. crushed pale malt

1 oz. crushed black malt

3 gallons water

12 oz. soft dark brown sugar

8 oz. blended honey

2 oz. Hallertau

1 oz. Goldings

2 oz. brewers' yeast

Chimay Recipe, continued

1. Raise the temperature of the water to 55° C, and stir in the crushed malt. Stirring continuously, raise the temperature to 66° C. Leave for 1.5 hours, occasionally returning the temperature back to this value.

2. Contain the mashed grain in a large grain bag to retrieve the sweet wort. Using slightly hotter water than the mash, slowly and gently rinse the grains to collect 3.5 gallons of extract.

3. Boil the extract with the hops and the sugar and the honey dissolved in a little water until the volume has been reduced to just over 3 gallons. Strain off and divide equally in 4 1-gallon jars. Fit airlocks.

4. When cool add the yeast, and ferment until the vigorous activity abates. Then siphon off into 3 1-gallon jars, filling each to the base of the neck.

5. It will take weeks to complete the fermentation, after which the beer should be racked again, taking with it a minute quantity of the yeast sediment.

6. Store for 6 months before bottling in primed beer bottle (0.5 teaspoon per pint).

7. Mature for 18 months before sampling.

I set out to ask as many brewers as possible how they make the sorts of beers in this book, about the choices they make along the way, and why they make those choices. I mailed questionnaires to more than a hundred breweries in Belgium, the Netherlands, the United States, and Canada. I built an Internet site where homebrewers could contribute information about how they brew, submit recipes, and suggest questions they would like to have answered.

The hunt for answers to those questions begins in Belgium by considering the history of monastic brewing and the environment in which Trappist breweries first operated. It would be fun to know what the beers they made in the 1800s drank like, but while today's Trappist beers may be offspring, they taste very different. Like *Designing Great Beers*, this book examines how the pioneers brew, and also how other brewers in Belgium make similar beers. After American brewers producing Belgian-style ales answer the same questions put to the Belgians, the book details the ingredients available to American brewers and how to use them. The goal, of course, remains to brew these beers successfully. Thus, the last chapters deal specifically with the concept of styles, offer tips for professional and amateur brewers, provide specific information about what works, and conclude with recipes and the thinking behind them.

Before considering the journey in more detail, here are four things to pay particular attention to along the way:

Attenuation. Belgian brewers talk often about making sure a beer is "digestible." Laurent Demuynck, a Belgian native who heads Duvel Moortgat USA, wasn't kidding when he said: "For breakfast, I put *Duvel* in my waffle batter … Lightens it up." *Duvel* or *Orval* or *Rochefort 8* perfectly complement *and* compliment a Belgian waffle loaded with whipped cream and strawberries. These beers are strong and full of flavor without being cloying. Mashing regimen, sugar, yeast, and fermentation management hold the secret. Just look at the apparent attenuation numbers in Chapter 2.

There's no "i" in sugar. Historical references to the use of "candi sugar" in Trappist breweries beginning in the 1920s don't describe the crystal rocks Americans call "Belgian candi sugar," but most often a dark caramel syrup. This creates confusion to the extent that we might be better off avoiding the term throughout this book. Common usage by American brewers makes that impossible, so when you see "candi sugar" in the following pages, it will usually refer to the rocklike hunks used by Americans rather than an ingredient found in Belgian recipes. When we discuss "candi sugar" in historical terms, meaning caramel syrup or a similar product, the difference should be clear.

Refermentation in the bottle. Only two Trappist beers are even sold on draft, all get fresh yeast when bottled, and most are carbonated at higher levels than previously has been assumed as typical for Belgian-style ales. Good bottle-conditioning depends on, you guessed it, proper attenuation.

Trappist is not a style, but an appellation. Trappist-brewed beers may be very strong or not so strong, light in color or dark. Set aside preconceptions about style when reading about how monastery brewers make beer. We'll get to "style" later.

In Part I of the book, we'll look specifically at how Belgian brewers make these beers.

A visit to seven essential breweries (Chapters 2 & 3). Because only six Trappist monasteries brew, and they package but fifteen beers for sale, we can focus on the breweries and each of those beers, then consider the others they inspired. No Trappist, however, produces the closely linked type of beer Michael Jackson dubbed "strong golden." That style was born at the Moortgat Brewery and connected to monastery beers through influential brewing scientist Jean De Clerck. Jackson wrote that the beer known as *Duvel* "is also a good example of a Belgian beer that is a style in itself, and widely imitated."

Abbeys, blondes, and independent spirits (Chapters 4 & 5). A surge in popularity in Trappist beers led scores of breweries to produce abbey beers (*abdijbier* or *bière d'abbaye* in Flemish and French, respectively). In some cases, monasteries commissioned commercial brewers to make beers for them; in others, commercial breweries staked out the use of an abbey's name, although the monastery is no longer active. Adding to the confusion, even more beers put *dubbel* and *tripel* on their labels.

Part II begins by visiting a cross-section of American breweries that produce Belgian-inspired beers. Then we'll review ingredients and processes used by both Belgian and American brewers, giving particular attention to yeast and fermentation.

American beers, Belgian roots (Chapter 6). Distributors sometimes approach New Belgium Brewing Company founder Jeff Lebesch with questions about esoteric beers such as *La Folie* or the abbey styles *Abbey* and *Trippel.* "They ask, 'Why do you keep making these?' " Lebesch said. "I tell them, 'because that's who we are.' " Brewing styles with roots in Belgium can be commercially viable, but talk to American brewer after American brewer about making such beers, and their passion for the beers becomes obvious. They are still learning themselves and are eager to share information.

From grain to bottle (Chapters 7-9). Before tackling the new and exciting, brewing with sugar and taming exotic yeasts, we'll review the basics. The overview includes Trappist water profiles, their malt choices, and mashing regimens. We'll pay particular attention to fermentation management. We know Westmalle and Westvleteren use the exact same yeast. Westmalle restrains the fermentation temperature throughout, holding it to 68° F (20° C). Fermentation at

Westvleteren usually rises to 80 to 84° F (28 to 29° C). Before you pitch, understand what you expect of your yeast.

In Part III, we turn to brewing. Whether you plan to brew "in style" or brew to inspiration, you should be armed for better brewing.

The "S" word (Chapter 10). Yvan De Baets puts it succinctly when it comes to discussing beer styles: "Making categories helps the human brain, but it also limits it. Descriptions don't necessarily take into account complexity." We'll visit the debate—make no mistake, we're talking about an in-your-face debate—about using the words "Belgian" and "style" in the same sentence. To understand Trappist, abbey, and other beers of this family, it helps to think about where in Belgium they originated, rather than that they were born in monasteries.

Style categories particularly help define what this book covers:
- Category 18 in the Beer Judge Certification Program style guidelines (*www.bjcp.org*). Beers called Belgian Strong Ales include blonde, dubbel, tripel, golden strong ale, and dark strong ale. Beers that would be entered in Category 16E, Belgian Specialty, are also included, but not every Belgian specialty beer.
- Belgian-style dubbel, tripel, pale strong ale, dark strong ale, and other Belgian-style ales according to the Brewers Association Beer Style Guidelines. The Association uses these categories for the World Beer Cup®. At the Great American Beer Festival®, dubbel, tripel, and other Belgian-style abbey ales are judged as Belgian-style abbey ales, while pale strong ales, dark strong ales, and other strong specialty ales compete as Belgian-style strong specialty ales.

What works: Recipes (Chapter 11). You shouldn't consider this a recipe book (more on that momentarily), but this is where you'll find recipes created by both professional and amateur brewers, and they explain their thoughts about recipe formulation and making the recipes work. We'll look one more time at numbers from commercial brewers, at guidelines, and at how some homebrewers successfully brew these styles.

So, what's not in the book? For starters, a primer on brewing beer or a glossary of brewing terms. If you recently drank your first dubbel at your local brewpub, ran out and bought bottles of *New Belgium Abbey* and *Westmalle Dubbel,* then decided you wanted to take up homebrewing to make something similar, you had better back up. You need to know something about brewing before you use this book to make beer. Plenty of excellent basic brewing books explain the basics of step-infusion mashing, or how to adjust your brewing water. More technical publications are available should you decide to dive into challenges like culturing yeast strains.

I haven't attempted to put together a complete list of commercial producers on either side of the ocean—there are simply too many. Sorry, but some elegant beers don't even get a mention.

As noted, you won't find a lot of recipes. Instead, I've tried to list ingredients and processes for a cross-section of beers within each style. Other tables reveal measurable differences between beers within a style (such as *Chimay White* and *Affligem Tripel*), illustrate in aggregate what sort of ingredients homebrewers use, or contrast homebrewed beers with commercial examples.

Why not more recipes? Homebrewer Gordon Strong (you'll read more from him in Chapter 10) points out just how many celebrity chefs write recipe books inviting readers to clone their popular restaurant dishes. We have shelves of such books in our house, as well as many homebrewing books with recipes. However, *Designing Great Beers* includes no recipes, and another book I keep close to my brew kettle, Randy Mosher's *The Brewer's Companion* (Alephenalia, 1995), also doesn't offer recipes. On the other hand, I find Mosher's most recent effort, *Radical Brewing* (Brewers Publications, 2004), inspiring, and that book bleeds recipes.

He and I discussed this via e-mail. He wrote: "I too am scornful of recipes, although it seems to be the main thing people want out of brewing (as well as cooking) books. I'd much rather empower people, but they've had all the artistic confidence pounded out of them."

Strong views recipes as a way of comparing approaches. Mosher agrees with that idea. "One way of looking at them is as examples of principles of formulation, kind of explain the parts and pieces," he wrote. Such has been my goal, with brewers not only providing recipes but the how and why behind them.

Oregon homebrewer Noel Blake, who was inspired by *Westvleteren 12* to brew a beer that won second prize in the National Homebrew Competition, contributes one of the recipes. His "dream beer" description, also inspired by *Westvleteren 12*, took another turn when Brewery Ommegang used the narrative in creating *Three Philosophers Ale*. You might say he has a way with words, and he's free with advice.

"Think like a Belgian, brew like a monk," he said. "That is, make a distinctive beer that is expressive rather than imitative, and dedicate yourself to it as if there is nothing else in life."

A Word About Color

Describing the color of these beers, particularly the darker members of the family, presents a challenge. Ray Daniels writes in *Designing Great Beers*: "The determination of beer and wort colors has been troublesome in the malt and brewing industries for at least one hundred years. Half a dozen techniques—each giving different results—have been used to assess the color of beer during the past fifty years. To make matters worse, at least two of these methods have been used at one time by brewers in North America and Europe, making for further variation in comparisons of beer color."

With the exception of *New Belgium Abbey*, all color measurements in the tables in this book were done in European laboratories using the EBC (European Brewing Convention) method (New Belgium Brewing also uses the EBC method). This technique reads absorbance in a 1-centimeter cuvette at the same wavelength as is used by the Standard Reference Method (SRM) in the United States. The method employed by the American Society of Brewing Chemists (ASBC) employs a spectrophotometer to assess the amount of light absorbed by beer in a larger one-half-inch glass cuvette when illuminated with light at a specific wavelength, generating what it refers to as an SRM measurement (also known as ASBC—same number).

To compare EBC and SRM, the EBC number is divided by 1.97, which you'll see on the tables. Results can be surprising. For instance, tests at De Proef Brouwerij show *Westvleteren 12* at 79 EBC, which equates to 40 SRM. We would expect a beer with such a number to appear black to opaque, but *Westvleteren 12* flashes a reddish hue at the edges. As with so many aspects of brewing Trappist and abbey beers, it can be best to set aside preconceptions. If the translation from EBC to SRM results in a number that seems high, open one of the originals before brewing and check the color.

Brewing in Belgium

one

Silence, Please

*I*nside the brewery café at the monastery of the Saint Benedictus Abbey of Achel, only a single food server and one monk putting items on his cafeteria tray remained when Marc Beirens opened the door and stepped into a chilly December evening.

Beirens, a businessman who has been visiting monasteries since he was a child, took a few strides into a terrace area that was once the abbey's courtyard. As the sky above turned from dark blue to black, he nodded back toward the brewery, located in a space that once housed the monastery dairy, then to a new gallery and gift shop to his right. Those buildings held pigs and more cattle, before it became obvious agriculture would not sustain the community.

"You should have seen this all a few years ago," he said, his voice bouncing lightly about an otherwise silent courtyard.

* * * * *

Earlier in the afternoon, Brother Benedict sat in his office well inside the monastery walls. With computers, printers, and fax machines at his side, he talked about the life of a monk.

"There is a very strong regimen," he said. "Prayer, work, study, lecture, the Bible." A major service at 4:30 in the morning is the first of seven daily prayers—four large prayers and three small ones. "We may miss a little prayer if we are working, but here almost everyone is together for all of the prayers," he said. The rule of Saint Benedict decrees that monks should live by the work of their hands. Brother Benedict oversees the economics of the monastery. "I'm here for the marketing," he said, making a list. "There's a monk who works in the kitchen, one who works in the garden. Of course, one in the brewery."

Around the world, the average number of monks living in monasteries has dwindled, and often the workforce is further depleted by age and poor health, but the reach of Trappists continues to grow. The total number of their monasteries has more than doubled, from 82 in 1940 to 169 at the beginning of the twenty-first century. During the same sixty years, the number of Trappist monks and Trappistine nuns decreased by about 15%; there are now slightly more than 2,500 monks and 1,800 nuns worldwide.

In Iowa Trappistine nuns support themselves by producing candy, while monks nearby build caskets. In Oregon Trappists warehouse wine, and in Massachusetts brothers make jams and jellies. You can order Trappist cheese or homemade bourbon fudge from the Abbey of Gethsemani in Trappist, Kentucky.

In Belgium Trappists brew and sell beer. They not only support themselves, but also subsidize other monasteries and a wide range of charities. Just as important to readers of this book, they brew some of the best beer in the world. "Our beer is so good, we don't have to do anything to sell it," Brother

Benedict said. "The Trappist drinker is there, and he wants his Trappist beer. He knows its quality."

Until 1998 Achel was the only one of Belgium's six Trappist monasteries without a brewery. Today its small brewhouse produces little more than 2,000 hectoliters a year (less than 1,600 barrels), most of it sold in the café. Brother Benedict talked about the revival with unbridled enthusiasm. Walking through the monastery, at one moment he would point out the historical significance of simple arched hallways, and in the next he would glance into the future, passing through a long dining hall where a hundred monks once took their meals, envisioning when it will become a reception area for guests seeking retreat.

The guesthouse currently has a capacity of thirty-five, and it often will be full. Guests are permitted to stay for up to a week. The monks don't expect visitors to attend all seven prayers, but "if they are here, they will live the life like a monk," Brother Benedict said. "People come here to find the silence, to find answers on the questions of their life. It seems these days more people need this."

The notion that Trappists take a vow of total silence is incorrect. Such a vow never existed, although there were strict rules about speaking. While those rules have eased, at some times and in some places silence still is expected. The purpose of silence is to give one space in which to pray, meditate, and read, and to allow others to do the same.

"We have two new monks this year," Brother Benedict said, bringing the community to seventeen. "We have young monks, 55 years of age, who are coming from the business world with new ideas."

Brother Benedict of Achel in Monk Martinus' shop.

The monastery itself is closed to the public, but families from both Belgium and the Netherlands make the surrounding area a destination, walking on country trails that lead from the parking lot, then meeting in the café. Monk Martinus' shop, which began selling Belgian chocolates and beer in 1970, has developed into a very well-stocked general store. One room features beer from all over Belgium, monastic and otherwise. Brother Benedict showed it off with pride.

"There is life to the abbey," he said, quickly heading off toward the gift shop, gesturing to an open area that will be converted for use as a day retreat. "There is a vision of the future. There is commerce going on."

* * * * *

Marc Beirens appreciates the importance of commerce to the monasteries, and that the six Trappist breweries are part of a larger family. He distributes a range of monastic products—beer is the best selling, but they include cookies, soap, vegetables, wine, and other goods—throughout Belgium and France. His father did the same. "I've been visiting monasteries since I was this high," he said earlier, holding his hand below his waist. That's why he understands something else about monasteries.

It was dark now, and the courtyard empty.

"I love the silence," Beirens said. "I used to have a friend who was a monk. He's gone now."

We walked along in silence.

"When he was 80 or so, I'd still call him. If I had a problem I could go see him. He didn't have to say anything and I'd feel better.

"All it took was silence."

MONASTIC BREWING TRADITION

Anneke Benoit, who until recently ran the Claustrum (an exhibition room) at Westvleteren, puts it most simply: "If there is no monastic life, there is no monastic beer." The Claustrum—housed within *In De Vrede*, a café owned by the Abbey of Saint Sixtus—provides visitors a look at, and unique feel for, life in the abbey across the road. The brothers sell their highly coveted beer only at the café and at the door of the brewery. "People don't get that," she said, continuing her thought. "All the time they want to know why the monks don't brew more beer."

This is not only true at Westvleteren. Back in 1981, Dom Albert van Iterson, then the brewing director at Rochefort, explained: "We are not swayed by the pressures of demand. The beer supports the abbey and four workers who work with us. We

Key Dates in Trappist and Monastery Brewing

530
The rule of Saint Benedict is written, and to this day remains the reason why monks brew and sell beer.

750
Charlemagne and his followers promote the Benedictine way of life and monastery brewing.

820
The Saint Gall Monastery brewery plan is drawn, providing a blueprint for other monasteries.

1098
The Order of Cistercians is founded, promoting a stricter set of rules than the Benedictines.

1132
Cistercian monks resurrect the Orval monastery abandoned by the Benedictine order.

1464
Cistercian monks take over an abbey at Rochefort previously occupied by nuns.

1656
Seeking a purer living of the rule of Saint Benedict, a stricter order of Cistercians begins in La Trappe, becoming known as Trappists.

1790
The French revolutionary government suppresses all monasteries, confiscating their property.

1802
Monks fleeing France with the idea of heading to America found a Trappist monastery at Westmalle.

1830
Belgium declares its independence from the Netherlands.

1836
Monks at Westmalle begin brewing.

1839
Brewing begins at Westvleteren, established as a monastery five years earlier.

1844
Monks from Westmalle start a monastery at Achel, and brewing begins in 1852.

1850
Monks from Westvleteren found the abbey at Chimay, and in 1862 start brewing beer and selling it to the surrounding community.

1899
Rochefort resumes brewing twelve years after monks from Achel re-established the abandoned monastery.

1919
The government prohibits the sale of spirits in bars and other public places, helping create demand for stronger beers.

1922
Westmalle begins using a dark sugar syrup (also called "candi sugar") in *Westmalle Dubbel*, making the beer stronger without bloating its body.

1925
Chimay trademarks ADS (Abbaye de Scourmont), the first Trappist trademark.

1932
Orval, rebuilt in 1926, resumes brewing with a brand new recipe.

1934
Westmalle completes construction of a modern brewery, begins selling *Westmalle Tripel*, the first pale Trappist beer.

Key Dates, continued

1946
The abbot at Westvleteren decides to de-emphasize brewing, and a deal is struck to have Saint Sixtus beer brewed under contract.

1948
Father Theodore isolates the famous Chimay yeast, brews the famous *Blue/Grand Réserve* as a Christmas beer.

1955
Monks at Rochefort begin brewing *Spéciale*, now called *Rochefort 8* and the last new beer introduced by Rochefort.

1962
A trade court in Ghent rules that only Trappist monasteries can use the appellation *Trappistenbier*.

1992
Westvleteren ends a 46-year contract brewing deal with Saint Bernardus and reassumes control over all the beer it sells. Saint Bernardus begins selling beers under its own name.

1998
Achel resumes brewing.

set the limits; we brew on Monday, Tuesday, and Wednesday, we bottle on Thursday. To meet demand, we would have to brew fifteen to twenty times a week. We are not a commercial organization and have no desire to become one. We are monks."[1]

Trappist beers, and the way monastery breweries make them, have changed substantially since the beginning of the

---

[1] Jef van den Steen, *Les Trappistes: Les Abbayes et Leurs Bières* (Brussels: Editions Racine, 2003), 123.

twentieth century, but the monks' philosophy about brewing stretches clear back to Saint Benedict.

Monastery breweries likely pre-date the rule of Charlemagne (742-814), and when large-scale production of beer in Europe began in the eighth and ninth centuries, monasteries led the way. They had the capital to build breweries and ongoing access to grain. Monks consumed most of the beer themselves, and served some travelers or other visitors. Their beers probably tasted much like those made in homes, where the bulk of brewing still took place. At one time as many as six hundred monastery breweries operated in Europe. What eventually set them apart was the scale and method of production. Their practices served as a model of development for commercial breweries.

According to historian Walter Horn, "Before the twelfth and thirteenth centuries, when brewing first emerged as a commercial venture, the monastery was probably the only institution where beer was manufactured on anything like a commercial scale."[2]

Charlemagne's followers promoted monastery life according to the rule of Saint Benedict, written about A.D. 530. It called on monks to be self-sufficient through their own labor, and it also required them to offer hospitality to travelers, making production of beer all but essential. With water unsafe to drink, they needed to serve beer or wine, and beer was well established as the beverage of choice in the Low Countries that later became Belgium and the Netherlands.

Trappists are members of the Order of Cistercians of the Strict Observance. Robert, abbot of the monastery of Molesme, north of Lyons in France, established the Order of Cistercians in

[2] Quoted in Richard Unger, *Beer in the Middle Ages and the Renaissance* (Philadelphia: University of Pennsylvania Press, 2004), 27.

1098 with other monks critical of the moral laxity of the Benedictines. He took with him twenty monks and started a monastery at Citeaux, also in France. The arrival of Saint Bernard and thirty companions in 1112 assured the future of the reformist group. The monks of this order came to be known as the "white monks," in contrast to the traditional Benedictines, who wore black.

Trappists emerged from another reform, begun at the Cistercian monastery of La Trappe (hence they are called Trappists) in France in 1656 under the leadership of Abbot Armand-Jean de Rancé. Seeking once more a purer living of the rule of Saint Benedict, de Rancé initiated a series of observances that harkened back to the austere rigors of earlier monasticism.

To all of the old rules, including daily manual labor, silence, and seclusion, he added abstinence from meat. Monks no longer follow this practice, but at the time it elevated the importance of beer, providing vitamins vital to Trappists' daily diets.

In 1790 the French revolutionary government suppressed all monasteries and religious houses in France, confiscating their property. Monks and other religious leaders were either guillotined, escaped into exile, or abandoned their religious status. The novice master of La Trappe, Augustin de Lestrange, fled France with twenty-one monks of his monastery and set up his community in a vacant Carthusian monastery in Switzerland.

When Napoleon's armies threatened to invade Switzerland, de Lestrange, together with his monks and nuns, journeyed all the way to Russia. They gradually made their way back toward France, and these Trappists revived former monasteries or established new ones. Some were in the region that would become Belgium when it first became a sovereign nation in 1830, and those abbeys still brew today.

Historically, monasteries set brewing standards, with their scale of production and often-better equipment providing an example for neighboring breweries. The church was central to higher learning; abbeys were places to study and also clearing-houses for information. Unfortunately, while a large body of information about medieval and Renaissance brewing exists, it tells us little about what the beers might have tasted like or the practicalities of how they were brewed.

One particularly useful artifact is the Saint Gall Monastery Plan, drawn up about 820, which served as a blueprint for other monastery breweries. The plan called for a monastery to have three breweries—one making beers for guests, a second for the brothers, and a third for pilgrims and the poor. Guests, noblemen, and royal officials drank a beer made from wheat and barley, while the others consumed one brewed from oats. The brewery making beer for pilgrims and paupers was only a little more than half the size of the one for the brothers. To satisfy all the needs for guests, paupers, and brothers, a monastery the size of the one in the ideal Saint Gall Plan would have had to produce about 350 to 400 liters of beer per day, almost what Chimay brewed just before World War I (an estimated 1,200 to 1,400 hectoliters in 1914).

The tradition of brewing different-quality beers for different customers persisted throughout the Middle Ages and Renaissance. By then monasteries had only one brewhouse, with the second and third runnings from a single mash used to make a weaker beer or beers. The terms double and triple may have grown from the practice.

Westmalle is the lone Trappist brewery to label its beers that way today, and Westmalle produces its *Dubbel* and *Tripel* with separate mashes. Only Westvleteren keeps touch with the custom of Saint Gall. When the monks brew *Westvleteren 8* and *12* on the same day, they start with a single mash. Most of the high-gravity first runnings go to the stronger (10.2% abv) *Westvleteren 12*, while the weaker final runnings fill the kettle for *Westvleteren 8*.

Why? Brothers Joris and Jos learned the practice from Brother Filip, the previous brewer. "That's our training," Brother Joris said. "The knowledge is passed on from brother to brother."

File that under tradition.

two

The Inspiration: Trappist Breweries

Westmalle began brewing beer in 1836, Westvleteren's brewing license dates to 1839, and Chimay started selling beer away from its door in 1862. Also in the 1860s, Achel produced a beer known for higher quality than others of its region. By 1870 physicians endorsed Chimay's *Bière Forte* for its healthy qualities. However, little in brewing literature indicates beers produced in Trappist abbeys were viewed as a different *style*, and only a small part of production went to outside sales.

That changed in the twentieth century. In 1900 Belgium was a country of 6.7 million people with 2,632 towns, 197,821 drinking establishments, and 3,223 breweries. The number of breweries dwindled to a little more than 2,000 by 1920 and not much more than 1,000 before World War II. Today only around 130 breweries remain. Although the population has grown to 10.4 million, domestic production is less than in 1910, and Pilseners account for 70% of beer sold. Trappist breweries expanded as other ale producers, often local and small, failed.

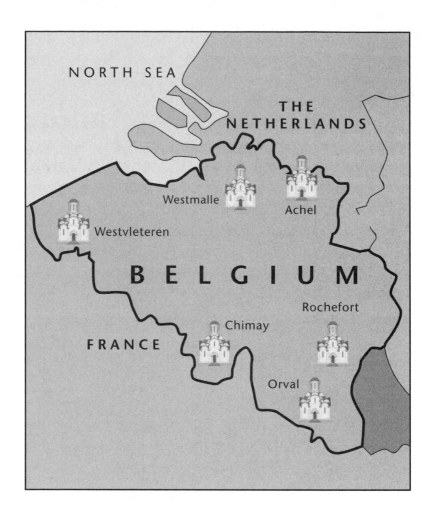

A Matter of Degrees

Until the early 1990s, Belgian brewers measured gravity in Belgian degrees. This could, and can, be calculated by subtracting 1 from a beer's specific gravity and multiplying by 100. Thus a 1.060 beer would be 6 degrees.

Today brewers measure in degrees Plato, but the beers may take their names from the former standard. Thus, Achel referred to its initial beers as *Blond 4* and *Bruin 5* when it resumed brewing. Westvleteren and Rochefort also call their beers by degree numbers as well as by the color of their crown caps.

Belgian law permits brewers more tolerance when listing alcohol content than in the United States. The listed content may vary by 1% alcohol by volume, compared to .3% in the States. That's one of the reasons that *Orval* labels state abv at 6.2% in Belgium and 6.9% in the United States. The variance at Orval is particularly relevant, because *Brettanomyces* continues to ferment the beer in the bottle, and *Orval* can reach 7.1%. Under Belgian law, a tax collector must have access to brewery records at any hour of the day. Often breweries set aside a small room and give the collector a key, allowing them entry to parts of monasteries where few but monks and brewery employees venture.

In this chapter, we'll visit the six monastery breweries. Each stop includes a monastery background, an overview of the beers produced, and a tour of the brewery with specific information about ingredients and brewing process.

Trappist breweries quickly joined the national effort at the beginning of the twentieth century to improve the quality and image of Belgian beers. Writing in *Belgium by Beer, Beer by Belgium*, Annie Perrier-Robert and Charles Fontaine note:

"Alarmed by the success of English beer in Belgium at the very beginning of the twentieth century, the teachers at the various brewery schools decided to create a 'Belgian' beer. The learned professor Henri Van Laer, in particular, had produced the idea that the country, famous for the diversity of its brewing production, should provide a type of modern beer capable of appealing to the most delicate palate."[1]

A contest in Brussels in 1902 for beers between 4.5 and 5 degrees Belgian (1.045 and 1.050, nearly twice as strong as most beers sold in Belgium at the time) attracted few entries, but a second one in 1904, called the "Contest for the Perfection of Belgian Beer," drew entries from seventy-three breweries. Products stemming from the contest were labeled "Belge."

Shortly after Rochefort resumed brewing in 1899, the abbey sent Father Dominique to the Catholic University at Leuven to learn about brewing, and by 1910 his beers were winning national awards.

Monastery breweries clearly benefited from the growing popularity of stronger beers, fueled in part by an invasion of foreign beers, and just as much by a prohibition on the sale of spirits (*genièvre*/gin) in bars and other public places. That law, enacted in 1919, also boosted the tax on beer, but that didn't deter consumers. "It was a signal for pubs to start selling bigger beer," said Philippe Van Assche, general manager at Westmalle. Westmalle likely created its *Tripel* in reaction, satisfying drinkers in the 1930s who wanted both stronger beer and one the color of trendy, light-colored Pilseners.

---

[1] Perrier-Robert and Fontaine, *Belgium by Beer, Beer by Belgium* (Luxembourg: Schortgen, Esch/Alzette, 1996), 88.

After rebuilding its brewery, which had been ransacked by Germans during World War I, Westmalle began actively selling beer. While the beer we now know as *Westmalle Dubbel* may have roots that go back to the 1850s, it changed several times over the years. In 1922 the brewery added caramelized sugar syrup called "candi sugar" to a recipe first used in 1909, raising the alcohol content and lightening the body. Although brewers in the Low Countries used sugar by the fifteenth century, they added it for flavor. When George M. Johnson wrote about Belgian brewing practices in 1916, he discussed the use of sugar, but reported nothing about breweries using sucrose or caramel syrup in the manner that Westmalle soon would.

Trappist beers of the 1920s weren't as strong as today, but they were stronger than other beers. As far back as the sixteenth century, brewers learned they could charge more for strong beer, considerably more than additional ingredients and labor would cost. Breweries in Jesuit houses in the Low Countries made beers called good and small, with the good having an alcohol content of about 5% and the small beer one of 2.5%. Beers took different names in different regions. In Ghent, for instance, *dubbele clauwaert* was introduced in 1573, and quickly supplanted *enekle clauwaert* as the best-selling beer. Commercial brewers often saw little value in producing a beer from second runnings, because the cost of goods and labor exceeded what they could charge for weaker beers. Well into the twentieth century, the Trappists had a built-in consumer base for their smaller beers, the monks themselves, making production of stronger beers more cost-effective. That changed as the need to supplement their diet with beer diminished and the number of members of each monastery dwindled, but by then the practice of using second runnings had pretty much disappeared as well.

The Trappists actively defended their mark after World War I. Chimay trademarked ADS (Abbaye de Scourmont) in 1925, Westmalle registered *Trappistenbier* in 1933, and Orval claimed rights to its image of a trout with a ring in 1934. In the 1930s and '40s the monks went to court several times in attempts to halt the sale of beers made by secular breweries but labeled Trappist. They scored an important victory in 1962, when a trade court in Ghent ruled that only Trappist monasteries could use the appellation *Trappistenbier*. The International Trappist Association later created an "Authentic Trappist Product" logo for beer and other products.

The Trappists defend their beers against other attacks just as quickly. In 2003, when the French instituted a 2-euro-per-liter tax on all beers above 8.5% abv, the Trappists joined with other Belgian brewers to get the tax scrapped. Various international news stories quoted spokesmen for the breweries. None may have been more effective than Father Omer, the monk officially in charge of brewing at Chimay, where the tax would have cost the monks $130,000 a month. Although Father Omer doesn't venture into the brewery itself every day and does none of the actual brewing, one syndicated story began that he "lifted his head from the huge vat where his beloved Trappist ale was brewing to address an issue which is vexing producers of Belgium's great beers. 'The French are playing tricks on us,' the soft-spoken monk said, before offering a more saintly thought. 'But, of course, we still love them.' "

Being a monk has its PR benefits.

ACHEL

The brewery at Achel offers a lesson in Trappist family relations. Founded by monks from Westmalle, Achel later sent monks to found the monastery at Rochefort. When Achel set out to resume brewing after a hiatus of more than seventy years, Brother Thomas, retired from Westmalle, wrote the recipes and did the initial brewing. After Brother Thomas' health failed, Brother Antoine, himself retired from Rochefort, took over and added new beers to the line. Marc Knops, a freelance brewer, has since taken charge, accepting the job after being recommended by Marc Beirens, distributor and sometimes confidante of all the monastery breweries.

Knops combined with Brother Antoine to refine the recipe for *Achel 8*, a tripel, and then the pair created *Achel Bruin Extra* together. Six years after its brewery opened, Knops said he suspected he was finished writing recipes at Achel. "I don't think you make changes when the product is good," he said. "At some other breweries I will experiment, make seasonal beers. In Achel, we continue what we are doing."

Table 2.1 Achel Beers

Beer	Original Gravity SG (°Plato)	Alcohol (abv)	Apparent Degree of Attenuation	Color SRM (EBC)	IBU
Blond 8 (Tripel)	1.078 (18.9 °P)	8.9%	84%	9 (18)	30
Bruin 8	1.079 (19 °P)	8.8%	83%	25 (50)	22
Bruin Extra	1.090 (21.5 °P)	10%	84%	30 (59)	28

Data provided by Derek Walsh; testing performed by De Proef Brouwerij and Westmalle. Color measured in EBC, converted to SRM by dividing by 1.97 (see p. 18).

That includes looking for ways to make its beer better. Because Achel does not have a bottling line, Knops and a monk who works in the brewery package 750ml bottles of *Extra* by hand. The 330ml bottles of *Blond 8* and *Bruin 8* must be sent off with yeast to another brewery for bottling. Early in 2005 Achel changed packaging partners, looking for more consistency. A couple of months earlier, Beirens and Brother Benedict talked about the need to make such decisions on a regular basis. "You are growing as the result of good quality," Beirens said.

Brother Benedict replied: "And every year we have to make it true. The last person to make the decision is the consumer." Brother Benedict has been at Achel less than three years, and he's not about to step into the brewhouse and go to work. Yet he is engaged with the beer, clearly a guardian of the brand. He had enjoyed some of the powerful *Extra* the night before, he said. When we went to the café to sample beer, he insisted we start with the *Extra*. He didn't drink himself, talking a little business with Beirens, answering my questions about the monastery, and excusing himself after his cell phone rang. He returned a little later. "This is the same bottle?" he asked, knowing the answer was yes. "You don't like the beer." He laughed mightily.

He insisted we have another, then headed off again. Both Beirens and I ordered the *Achel 5*, a blonde beer of 5.3% abv, and compared it to the 5% abv *Westmalle Extra*. When Brother Benedict returned, he looked at our blonde beers, working on a scowl. He took a sip of one. "Water," he said, once again laughing. Of course, he didn't have to drive home.

Background
Achel, in northwest Belgium, literally straddles the border between Belgium and the Netherlands. In fact, when the monks take meals, some may be eating in Belgium, the others in the

Netherlands. "We say we are living in Belgium, graved in the Netherlands," Brother Benedict said, referring to the fact that the graveyard and surrounding gardens are across the (invisible) border. Belgium did not yet exist when religious hermits first built a chapel in the area in the seventeenth century. Not long after Belgium became independent (1830), monks from Westmalle established a monastery on the site in 1844. A brewery and malting operation were in place by 1852, although the monks probably produced beer only for themselves, replacing what they previously bought from local brewers.

The monks soon brewed a beer called *Patersvaatje* ("the small barrel of the father"), described as a strong beer of 12 degrees. Although accounts praise it for its strength and quality, it seems more likely it was 1.048 (12 °P) than 12 degrees Belgian (1.120). Tax records indicate the monks brewed only one day a month. After the Germans destroyed the brewery in

Achel's brewhouse is on display behind glass in a café run by the monastery, making it the only Trappist brewery open to the public.

World War I, the monastery made plans to rebuild but eventually abandoned them.

When the monastery opened a shop selling Belgian chocolates and beer in 1970, visitors asked to buy beer from the abbey itself. Achel struck a deal with Pierre Celis at De Kluis Hoegaarden to rename his *Vader Abt* beer as *Trappistenbier van De Achelse Kluis. Trappistenbier* was removed from the name following protests. After De Kluis burned in 1985, production went first to Sterckens Brewery and then Brewery Den Teut, before Achel decided to open its own brewery. The monks sold off some of the land around the abbey to raise about a half-million dollars and opened the first Trappist brewpub in 1998.

Beers

Brother Thomas initially created three beers for Achel: *Blond 4, Bruin 5,* and *Blond 6,* all-malt beers clearly inspired by *Westmalle Extra,* another of his recipes. Brother Thomas described the *Blond 4* as suited for "walkers and cyclists" (both popular activities for Achel visitors). He used only Pilsener malt, and hopped the beer with Kent Goldings, Hallertau-Hersbrucker, and Saaz in five additions, for an estimated 33 to 37 units of bitterness. The *Blond 4* has since become a *Blond 5,* while the *Bruin 5* remains, with both served on draft at the brewery café.

Brother Antoine added the *Achel Bruin 8* and the *Achel Blond 8,* the latter a tripel, first brewed in 2001. Knops, who brews an excellent tripel for *Brasseurs-Brouwers* on the Grand'Place in Brussels, worked on the recipe with Brother Antoine, who previously brewed only dark beers at Rochefort. They designed it with the idea it would undergo refermentation in the bottle,

Achel Bruin Extra

Original Gravity: 1.090 (21.5 °P)

Alcohol by Volume: 10%

Apparent Degree of Attenuation: 84%

IBU: 28

Malts: Pilsener, chocolate

Adjuncts: Sucrose, dark caramel syrup

Hops: Saaz

Yeast: Westmalle

Primary Fermentation: Yeast pitched at 63 to 64° F (17 to 18° C), climbs to 72 to 73° F (22 to 23° C), 7 to 8 days

Secondary Fermentation: 3 to 4 weeks at 32° F (0° C)

Also Noteworthy: Refermentation in the bottle with Westmalle yeast

although circumstances kept them from doing that for the first batch. "It became much better after we did," Knops said. Brother Antoine and Knops later collaborated on a dark, strong Christmas beer called *Extra*. "It was very good, so we decided to make it all year," Knops said. Because a merchant in the Netherlands took some of the first batch of *Extra* and renamed it *De Drie Wijzen* (the Three Wise Men) for the holidays, there was some confusion when *Extra* became a regular offering, although anything other than the simplest name is not Trappist-like.

Back in his office, Brother Benedict lifted a bottle of the *Bruin Extra* from a box. The brewery briefly used more stylized labels, then returned to the original design. "Our color should not be too beautiful," Brother Benedict said. "It is monastic. Sober."

Brewery

Achel uses Dingemans malts, plus whole flower Saaz hops acquired from Westmalle. Knops describes the water as soft and uses it as is. In theory, the brew length measures 15 hectoliters, but Knops expects to have more like 10 to 11 hectoliters at the end of the boil. He conducts a step mash, letting it rest 15 minutes at 118° F (48° C), 20 minutes at 144° F (62° C) with some variation, and until saccharification at 162° F (72° C), then mashing out at 174° F (79° C). Filtering takes 2 hours, and the boil lasts 90 minutes.

Knops puts only Pilsener malt and white sugar in the tripel, while the *Bruin* includes Dingemans Roost 900 (basically a chocolate malt) as well. The *Bruin Extra* features more of everything, plus caramelized sugar. Knops adds almost all the Saaz hops at the beginning of the boil.

Like Westvleteren, Achel uses freshly harvested yeast from Westmalle, picked up on brewing day. Beer ferments in 30-hectoliter (25.5-barrel) cylindro-conicals within the brewery or one 50-hectoliter (42.5-barrel) tank outside. Fermentation begins at 63 to 64° F (17 to 18° C) and climbs to 72 to 73° F (22 to 23° C) during fermentation. Primary fermentation lasts five to six days for *Achel Blond* and *Bruin* and seven to eight for the *Extra*. The former are transferred to a lagering tank and spend two to three weeks at 32° F (0° C). The *Extra* remains in its original tank, where it sits three to four weeks at 32° F (0° C).

Refermentation in the bottle takes two to three weeks at 72 to 73° F (22 to 23° C).

Knops might spend four days at Achel one week and none the next. When he brews, he and Brother Jules, the only monk to work in the brewery, sometimes make up to four batches in a row. "I brew, then he takes over while I go sleep for a few hours," said Knops, who is in his 40s. "I will rest when I am on pension." Brother Jules monitors fermentation throughout the week. Achel has a small lab but leans on the Westmalle lab for help with any problems beyond the ordinary.

Secular brewers oversee day-to-day operations at five of the six Trappist breweries, but none of the others also puts in time at other breweries. Knops gains a unique perspective visiting the range he tours. "I like to brew everywhere," he said. "But the monastery is something else I cannot explain. I cannot find the word. It's like you go to a castle ... it's another world."

CHIMAY

For most beer drinkers around the world, Chimay means Trappist beer. Chimay became the first monastery to sell beer away from its door, the first to bottle, and the first to promote the Trappist mark. It sells beer in more countries than any other Trappist brewery, and exports the largest percentage of its production (120,000 hectoliters, or 102,000 barrels), about 35%.

When beer writer Michael Jackson spotlighted Trappist beers in the 1970s and 1980s, Chimay's Father Theodore made an excellent brand representative. He spoke at length in Jackson's *Beer Hunter* television series about how he refined the Chimay yeast in 1948:

"I, myself. Painstaking work, requiring Benedictine patience. I isolated a certain number of cells, and out of these I selected and grew those which were most suitable for our type of beer. In order to make our beer, there were many things to consider. Firstly, it had to taste nice, it had to have a good taste, of course. Secondly, we have a beer with high specific gravity, and many yeast strains die when the alcohol concentration is too high. They stop fermenting.

Table 2.2 Chimay Beers

Beer	Original Gravity SG (°Plato)	Alcohol (abv)	Apparent Degree of Attenuation	Color SRM (EBC)	IBU
Dorée (Refter)	1.040 (10 °P)	4.6%	87%	8 (16)	16
Red	1.061 (14.9 °P)	7.1%	88%	15 (30)	19
White (Tripel)	1.069 (16.9 °P)	8.2%	89%	8.5 (17)	35
Blue	1.077 (18.7 °P)	9%	89%	40 (80)	35

Data provided by Derek Walsh; testing performed by De Proef Brouwerij. Color measured in EBC, converted to SRM by dividing by 1.97 (see p. 18).

"So, the yeast had to be more resilient to alcohol. Next, and most importantly, we ferment our beer in the bottle. So the yeast, when we put it in the bottle, must sink to the bottom and not remain in suspension."[2]

Father Theodore began working in the brewery in the 1940s, and even after he officially retired in 1991 would attend the daily sensory evaluation session, drinking a glass of *Chimay White* for pleasure. He and Chimay enjoyed a particularly strong relationship with famed brewing scientist Jean De Clerck, whom Father Theodore credited with introducing scientific practice to the Chimay brewery. De Clerck often sent promising brewing students to study at Chimay. He is buried on the grounds.

[2] Jackson, *The Beer Hunter: The Burgundies of Belgium.* VHS (Bethesda, Md.: The Discovery Channel, 1989).

Including the brewery, bottling plant, and marketing, eighty-two people work for Bières de Chimay. Chimay began producing cheese in 1876, bathing the rind of one in beer, and now sells Chimay cheeses in many countries. Overall, Chimay employs more than one hundred and fifty people, making it one of the biggest employers in one of Belgium's poorest regions. A part of the profits from brewing and cheese production go to help or build other Cistercian monasteries, with the rest dedicated to various projects in the area of Chimay. Twenty monks live at the monastery.

Background

Monks dispatched from Westvleteren in 1850 established the Abbaye de Scourmont, within easy walking distance of the French border. The monastery commands a hillside, amid trees and surrounding farmland, regal in a manner that makes it hard to imagine it was hacked out of marshland and forest. Monks toiled for twelve years in harsh conditions to complete the abbey, and by then a brewery was up and running, with immediate sales to the public. The first beer, produced in 1862, was called *Bavaria* and was described as a bottom-fermented beer such as those from Dortmund in Germany. A strong brown ale, perhaps drawing on a recipe from Westvleteren, replaced that after only a few batches. The monks drank a weaker table beer served from wooden casks, bottled *Bière Forte* ("strong beer") in a cellar under the kitchen, and promoted the product sold in 750ml bottles as Trappist-made.

Beginning in 1875 Chimay offered the public two kinds of beer, with the only difference being that the higher-priced one was aged in tar-coated barrels.

Doctors endorsed the beer from tarred barrels as healthier. Chimay continued to emphasize the quality of its beer when the brewery was rebuilt after being sacked by the Germans in World War I. By calling the first beer available after the war "intermediate," the monks assured that a strong beer would command a higher price after undergoing a lengthy cellaring.

Beers

The color of the caps on beers sold in 330ml bottles identify the three beers offered for sale. They carry different names than on the 750ml bottles: *Chimay Red* (*Première*), inspired by *Bière*

Chimay Red

Original Gravity: 1.061 (14.9 °P)

Alcohol by Volume: 7.1%

Apparent Degree of Attenuation: 88%

IBU: 19

Malts: Pilsener, caramel

Adjuncts: Wheat starch, sugar

Hops: Bittered with American hops, flavored with Hallertau

Yeast: Chimay

Primary Fermentation: Pitched at 68° F (20° C), rises to 81 to 82° F (27 to 28° C), 4 days

Secondary Fermentation: 3 days at 32° F (0° C)

Also Noteworthy: Refermentation with primary yeast

Forte, can fairly be called a dubbel; the *White* (*Cinq Cents*) a tripel, and the *Blue* (*Grande Réserve*) a dark strong. The *Blue* began as a Christmas specialty in 1948, eventually becoming a year-round product in 1954. The strongest of the family at 9% abv, the *Grande Réserve* draws comparisons to port when properly cellared. Chimay also packages *Grande Réserve* in magnum bottles.

The brewery makes a beer for the monks, called *Dorée* or *Refter*, three or four times a year. Unlike the other beers, whose spicy characteristics can be attributed to the yeast, *Dorée* contains coriander and curaçao. *Auberge de Poteaupré*, the inn the monastery operates about a quarter mile from the abbey, sells *Dorée*, and the beer sometimes shows up in beer cafés away from the brewery.

Brewery

After the Germans sacked the brewery again in World War II, the monks decided not only to rebuild and expand, but to modernize and improve quality controls. Father Theodore and De Clerck worked together, and by all accounts the monk took a hands-on role in the brewery for more than forty years. He wasn't afraid to make changes. According to Chimay records, he first began using hop extracts in 1950. When he developed the recipe for *Chimay White* in 1966, he used only hop extracts, well before most smaller breweries used extracts.

In 1967 Father Theodore totally replaced flowers and pellets in *Chimay Red* and *Chimay Blue* with extracts. Later he told a visiting brewer that he made the change because extracts gave him more control over bitterness from batch to batch. Two other Trappist breweries, Orval and Westvleteren, have since begun using extracts, and today we find extracts at many of the larger breweries producing abbey-type beers. "I don't know lots of small brewers who use them," said Marc Knops, the brewer at Achel who has worked in many other breweries as well. "Most of them use pellets. They give you a better flavor."

Father Theodore oversaw multiple brewery additions and renovations beginning in the 1960s and into the 1990s, including installation of cylindro-conical tanks that replaced open fermenters. The tanks, holding 500 hectoliters (425 barrels), measure 8 meters deep and 4 meters wide with a shallow cone, maximizing the amount of beer exposed to the yeast, according to the brewery.

Chimay takes its water from its own well, and illustrated how much it values the quality during one round of expansion. The brewery briefly contracted with La Trappe, then considered a Trappist monastery, to produce *Chimay White*. To ensure consistency, Chimay shipped water to the brewery in the Netherlands for La Trappe to use in brewing the *Chimay White*. De Clerck once declared the water perfect for brewing. The brewery calls it soft and low in minerals, particularly low in calcium and magnesium.

Chimay, which had its own maltings until after World War II, now uses malt produced in Belgium, with much of the barley grown in France. Michael Jackson has reported that six-row winter barley is malted to Chimay's high-enzyme specification. Because of six-row's higher enzyme content, more protein, less starch, and a thicker husk, most craftbreweries prefer two-row. However, the higher level of diastatic enzymes makes six-row barley desirable for conversion of adjunct starches during mashing, which the brewer who followed Father Theodore told a reporter Chimay uses.

In 1999 Casimir Elsen wrote in *Den Bierproever* that Chimay included a substantial amount of wheat starch in brewing *Chimay White*, citing a recipe he was given by Father Thomas, the monk in charge of brewing at the time. Elsen reported that he was told the grist for *Chimay White* was 66% malts by weight, 22% wheat starch, and 12% sugar. The brewery has denied several times using wheat starch, saying that wheat flour (10 to 15% of the grist) is used for head retention, and that recipes have not changed since first written by Father Theodore.

Father Thomas, who took over for Father Theodore, was featured in Chimay advertising in the 1990s.

Philippe Henroz, Chimay's marketing and communications manager, said the recipe printed in *Den Bierproever* "is absolutely not a recipe for the *Chimay White*." He said the brewery does not want to offer an official response to "every story that we can read on the Internet. We just want to say that we use only natural ingredients, and that we respect the way of production elaborated by Father Theodore." He said that mistranslation of ingredients has led to misunderstandings about changes at Chimay.

Quality control manager Dominque Denis said that the brewery discontinued using candi sugar (the syrup) about forty years ago. He said sugar amounts to less than 5% of fermentables.

Bittering hops have varied over the years, usually coming from the Yakima Valley and including Cluster, Galena, and Nugget. German Hallertau hops are used for flavor.

Fermentation begins at 68° F (20° C) and rises to 81 to 82° F (27 to 28° C). Temperatures sometimes reached 93° F (34°

C) before the brewery improved cooling, and beer quality suffered even though Father Theodore selected the yeast strain with temperature in mind. After four or five days of primary fermentation, beer is centrifuged and spends just three days in secondary at 32° F (0° C).

Workers centrifuge beer again after secondary, then dose it with sugar and the primary yeast before putting it in a tanker truck and transporting it to nearby Baileux, where a bottling plant was built away from the abbey so it wouldn't disturb the monks.

ORVAL

Producing but one beer, it might seem that the monks of Abbaye d'Orval operate with a particularly singular purpose. Of course, it's not that simple. Balancing the operation of the variety of

Orval, best shown from the air, might be a little larger than some other Trappist monasteries. Twenty or fewer monks now live in quarters that once housed more than a hundred. Photo courtesy of Orval.

commercial endeavors at Orval with a life of prayer challenges twenty-first century monks more than when the rule of Saint Benedict was written.

Orval dominates the appropriately named Valley of Gold, well to the south of Belgium and quite near the French border. More than 100,000 visitors a year tour ruins of the twelfth-century abbey or seek retreat in the guest rooms. Many visit the gift shop to buy cheese, bread, beer, and other products made by Trappists and Trappistines. Overall, sixteen monks live in the monastery once inhabited by a hundred.

In the 1990s Jacques Petre left the business world to run brewery operations at Orval. Interviewed at the time, he explained why he took the job rather than others he was offered. "I wanted to try and live like a Christian, but it's not easy in the business world. This job gave me the chance."

Table 2.3 Orval Beers

Beer	Original Gravity SG (°Plato)	Alcohol (abv)	Apparent Degree of Attenuation	Color SRM (EBC)	IBU
Petit	1.024 (6 °P)	3.4%	98%	14 (28)	21
Orval	1.055 (13.6 °P)	6.8%	94%	9 (22)	38

Data provided by Derek Walsh; testing performed by De Proef Brouwerij. Color measured in EBC, converted to SRM by dividing by 1.97 (see p. 18).

Petre immediately found challenges. "There are a lot of contradictions between the two worlds," he said. The monks told him that cutting costs shouldn't mean eliminating lay jobs or reducing salaries. "Before anything happens, you have to explain it to the monks; you have to explain it to the board; you have to explain it to the workers; you have to explain it to everybody. It takes time, and for a monk time doesn't exist in the way it does for most people," he said.[3]

Background

Orval qualifies as the oldest monastery occupied by current Trappists, and the youngest. Benedictines founded it in 1070, but abandoned it shortly thereafter, leaving Cistercians to re-establish the abbey in 1132. The first record of brewing at the monastery dates to 1628, but it seems likely monks made beer there as early as the twelfth century. The monastery became Trappist in the seventeenth century, then returned to the more mainstream Cistercian order in the eighteenth century. Like other monasteries, the French sacked it in the 1790s, and it was not rebuilt until 1926.

Legend has it that the princess Mathilda gave Orval its name. When her wedding ring fell into a lake in the valley, she prayed for its return. At once a trout rose to the surface with the precious ring in its mouth. Mathilda exclaimed: "Truly this place is a Val d'Or'! ("Valley of Gold")." In gratitude, she decided to establish a monastery on the site. Orval trademarked its logo showing a trout with a golden ring in 1934.

Beers

Tim Webb has described *Orval* as "God's home-brew."

The brewery lays no claim to having re-created an ancient recipe when brewing resumed in 1932. The first brewer came from Germany and his assistant from East Flanders. For whatever the reason, they created a recipe like no other Trappist beer.

---

[3] Gordon Young. "Free Market Monks in the 20th Century." *Beer the Magazine* 2, no. 3 (September 1994): 31.

Françoise de Harenne, Orval's commercial director, believes the recipe of today is little different than the first, and thus would have been dry-hopped from the outset. Of course, we also associate the famous *Goût d'Orval* (the taste of *Orval*) with *Brettanomyces*, wild yeast which not only adds a fresh leather taste but also consumes sugars other yeast do not, lightening and firming the body.

Michael Jackson writes that the Flemish brewer may have introduced *Brettanomyces*. When De Clerck, who also played instrumental roles in making Chimay and Rochefort beers what they are, consulted with the brewery in 1950, he suggested the beer stone that had built up in the lagering tanks be scrubbed out. After customers complained that *Goût d'Orval* had been lost, brewers collected wild yeast strains of the area, which have been added to secondary fermentation ever since.

Orval certainly shares many flavor characteristics with the saison-style beers of the surrounding region, not only because saisons in the 1930s were more likely to be influenced by wild yeasts but because they are also brewed with water high in bicarbonate.

Although the brewery distributes only *Orval*, it produces *Petit Orval* (also called *Orval Vert*) for the monks and to sell in the brewery's café. A modest 3.4% abv, *Petit* is made about three times a year by adding the regular *Orval* mother wort to a secondary tank with water already in place.

Brewery

Monks started the brewery in order to raise money to rebuild the monastery, and for the first twenty years only lay people worked within it. "The brewery was not created for giving the monks an activity," de Harenne said. Today, thirty-two lay workers produce about 45,000 hectoliters (38,300 barrels) of beer a year. The brewery operates as a separate financial entity that leases the Orval name from the monastery, with the monks controlling the company. Each month, the private company pays a percentage of sales to the abbey, with 55% of that given to charity and the remainder used to maintain the monastery.

The brewery looks like any other building in the monastery complex, although on a chilly winter morning steam billowing from a brew that begins each day at 5 a.m. gives the location away. Many days a second brew starts at 1:30 p.m. and lasts until 11 p.m. Mashing and boiling take place on the second floor of the classic brewhouse, in glistening copper kettles.

Orval adjusts the pH of its water, hard and high in bicarbonate. In 1993 the brewery lowered boiling pH from 5.2 to 5.0, creating a smoother bitterness. When he tasted the lower level of bitterness shortly thereafter, beer activist Yvan De Baets began a campaign that was still going on twelve years later. He's not the only one to notice a change. Beer writer Michael Jackson noted, "(the water) no doubt heightens the firmness and bitterness of the beer, though that has diminished a little in recent years."[4]

De Baets said Jean-Marie Rock, the secular brewer in charge since the 1990s, mapped out the change for him during a conversation in 2004, literally drawing De Baets a picture of how he expected drinkers to perceive a smooth bitterness compared to a harsher (and in the case of *Orval*, classic) bitterness associated with high carbonate water. "I give him credit. He is a man of character, and I have respect for him," De Baets said. "He claims

[4] Jackson, *The Great Beers of Belgium* (London: Prion Books, 2001), 234.

that it only affects post-bitterness, but you know it will affect not only the bitterness."

Rock disagrees. "pH adjustment has a very low influence on the beer quality," he said. "I don't understand why everybody is focusing only on details. It is impossible to produce a good beer with details."

The recipe includes three pale malts and two caramel malts. Rock decides on the malts each year after tasting samples. "When you are cooking, you make first the choice of the raw materials, and then you try to find good equipment to achieve a good preparation," Rock explained. "During the preparation,

Orval

Original Gravity: 1.055 (13.6 °P)

Alcohol by Volume: 6.8%

Apparent Degree of Attenuation: 94%

IBU: 38

Malts: 3 pale malts, 2 caramel malts

Adjuncts: Clear liquid candi sugar (about 16% of fermentables)

Hops: Styrian Goldings, Hallertau

Yeast: Orval

Primary Fermentation: Yeast is pitched at 57° F (14° C), may rise to 72° F (22° C), 4 days

Secondary Fermentation: 3 weeks at 59° F (15° C) with new yeast (including *Brettanomyces*) and Styrian Goldings flowers

Also Noteworthy: Refermentation in the bottle with primary yeast for 5 weeks at 59° F (15° C); centrifuged, but *Brettanomyces* remains and will continue to ferment

you taste a lot of the time. You add some salt and pepper or other aroma enhancer. You try to get the preparation at the good temperature without burning it at all. And finally you choose the best to go with."

Speaking more specifically about beer, Rock said, "I don't want the pale malt to be too soft. Let the softness come from the crystal."

Orval mashes at 145° F (63° C) for a "variable" time, and then boosts the temperature to 162° F (72° C) for 20 minutes. Lautering lasts about three hours. Brewers add Styrian Goldings and Hallertau hops from Slovenia and Bavaria 20 minutes into a 60-minute boil. The brewery used whole flowers in the kettle into the 1990s before shifting to a combination of hop extract and pellets. Liquid candi sugar provides 16 to 17% of fermentables.

Orval finished converting to cylindro-conical fermenters in 2004, shortening primary fermentation from five days to four.

The brewery began to migrate fermentation from open stainless steel fermenters to 200-hectoliter (170-barrel) cylindro-conical tanks in the late 1990s. Workers mounted a single tank, conducted taste tests and made adjustments, based mostly on sensory analysis. "When you change something, you have to know what you do," Rock said. "You have to know how to produce beer, to have some idea of the technology, and to taste and taste again and again."

The brewery put five more cylindro-conical tanks on line in 2004, after "nobody was able to recognize which beer came from where," de Harenne said. Modernization continues at a regular pace. Orval added a new lagering cellar, with six 200-hectoliter tanks and the distinctive trout-and-ring logo set in tile in the floor, in 1998. It replaced its 22-year-old bottling line in 2005, and began working on plans to install a new brewhouse in 2008. "The monks don't hesitate to invest," de Harenne said. "Usually in the monasteries you will find splendid equipment."

By turning to cylindo-conicals tanks, Orval shortened primary fermentation from five days to four. Fermentation begins at 57° F (14° C) and may rise to 72° F (22° C) during the four days. "We play with the temperature a bit," de Harenne said. The brewery uses the same yeast for sixteen generations.

Secondary fermentation takes place at 59° F (15° C) in horizontal tanks for three weeks. The beer is dry-hopped with flowers. These have varied over the years, as Rock prefers Styrian Goldings, while his predecessor used East Kent Goldings. More important, Orval adds a second yeast "of the area." The yeast contains multiple strains, including one of *Brettanomyces*.

Until recently the beer was neither filtered nor centrifuged. Now the brewery uses a centrifuge before bottling, to remove much of the old yeast, then doses the beer inline with sugar and the primary yeast. Enough *Brettanomyces* remains in the bottle that fermentation continues, although the brewery calculates refermentation will last only nine months. About 3 million cells of fresh yeast are added per milliliter, with a target of 10 grams of carbon dioxide (5 volumes) per liter in the bottle. In comparison, De Koninck pale ale contains about 4.8 grams per liter.

Lasting five weeks, refermentation in the bottles takes longer than at other monasteries because the cellars are not nearly as warm, 59° F (15° C). Down to the bottle and its serving glass, *Orval* remains a little different. Henry Vaes, the architect who designed Orval's modern monastery, also created the skittle-shaped bottle and a unique chalice.

"When I drank *Orval* beer for the first time ... I was impressed by its mysterious something," said Father Lode, the former managing director of the brewery. "I remember saying to myself, this is really an art, and art is something important to me. Beer is not something that comes from throwing a few ingredients together," he said, using his hands to illustrate. "It demands a lot from people. ... I admire the people who work here."[5]

ROCHEFORT

Abbaye Notre-Dame de Saint-Rémy just outside of Rochefort, in a particularly picturesque area of the Ardennes, has a monastic history stretching back nearly eight hundred years, a brewing tradition at least four hundred years old, and if you were to choose a single Trappist brewery to be put in a time capsule to

[5] Orval. *A Visit to the Orval Brewery*. DVD. Villers-devant-Orval: Ripley/Orval, 2002.

be opened a thousand years from now would be a fine representative for all the abbeys. When modern brewing began in 1899, workers ground malt in a water mill and hauled it to the brewery. They heated kettles with wood, and mashing took three men seven hours of continuous work. To regulate the temperature, they built a fire in a wagon that could be pushed under the vessels, then removed. The monks weren't concerned about producing a commercially viable product, just a supplement for their vegetarian diet.

Beer quality improved after the abbey sent Father Dominique to the Catholic University at Leuven to learn about brewing. In 1910 his work won a Grand Prix award at an exhibition in Brussels. Soon the abbey began bottling and selling beer, producing about 350 hectoliters (300 barrels) in 1920. Not until after World War II did brewing become the major source of income, but the course was set.

Today, seventeen monks live at Rochefort, and six participate in brewing, along with lay workers. Profits from selling beer funded recent construction on new reception and meeting

Table 2.4 Rochefort Beers

Beer	Original Gravity SG (°Plato)	Alcohol (abv)	Apparent Degree of Attenuation	Color SRM (EBC)	IBU
Rochefort 6	1.072 (7.5 °P)	7.8%	83%	20 (40)	18
Rochefort 8	1.078 (19 °P)	9.2%	90%	32 (63)	22
Rochefort 10	1.096 (23 °P)	11.3%	89%	45 (90)	27

Data provided by Derek Walsh; testing performed by De Proef Brouwerij. Color measured in EBC, converted to SRM by dividing by 1.97 (see p. 18).

rooms, and the bottom of an old filtering tank is set in one. Beer sales paid for remodeling a magnificent church, open for public services, in the mid-1990s. The ceiling and walls come from the stone blocks of old farmhouses in the Loire Valley, and the windows are filled with slabs of alabaster.

Background

Nuns founded an abbey in 1230 as Le Secours Notre-Dame, and Cistercian monks took it over in 1464. Brewing could have begun almost immediately, although written records note no activity until 1595, when the brewer also ran the mill. Most monastery records were lost when the abbey fell victim to the French Revolution, but engravings remain that show old hop gardens.

Victor Seny, a retired army chaplain who wanted to fund an abbey and become an abbot (its leader), revived the Saint-Rémy abbey. After he acquired the land the monastery once occupied, as well as some remaining buildings, he approached two abbeys about sending monks for his new monastery. Achel became the mother house of Rochefort. Father Anselme, the prior of the new priory, came from Achel in 1887 with a predisposition toward brewing. Seny did not become the abbot; instead, he joined the monastery as a monk.

Beers

Rochefort modeled its first beer on Achel's *Patersvaatje*. The abbey produced two beers, a refectory (table) beer for the monks and a stronger beer, probably about 3.5 degrees Belgian (1.035), to be sold to the public. The strength of that beer varied, because the Germans put a cap on beer strength when they occupied Belgium during both world wars. The brewery made a small quantity of 5-degree (1.050) beer for the sick during World War II, and began selling this beer to the public after the war ended. Sales initially soared, and by 1949 the abbey had acquired a truck to make home deliveries.

Success didn't last. When Rochefort had to rebuild its brewery following World War I, Chimay helped install new parts, but by 1950 the monastery ally became a competitor. After Father Theodore began to make improvements in the Chimay beers, consumers bought them instead of Rochefort's. Sales dropped so dramatically that Rochefort didn't produce enough spent grain to feed the abbey's cattle. Rochefort's abbot asked Chimay to stop selling beer near Rochefort. Chimay declined, instead offering to help Rochefort improve its beers. In the following two years, Jean De Clerck consulted on changes, a new brewer trained with Chimay at its Scourmont brewery, and Rochefort rolled out new recipes.

De Clerck first focused on brewing practices, including regular microbiological tests and better sanitation. He insisted that a stable and manure pile near the brewery be moved. Modernization of the brewhouse—equipment from 1902 was still being used in 1950—has been ongoing pretty much since.

The monks created a new strong beer called *Merveille* and retooled the refectory beer. *Rochefort 10* grew out of *Merveille*. The abbey first sold *Rochefort 6* in 1953, then in 1955 added its last beer, called *Spéciale* then and *Rochefort 8* now. Rochefort eliminated the monks' beer in 1973, because it made no sense to brew and bottle the small quantities needed. The new recipes took some inspiration from Chimay, which also initially provided its yeast, but the beers quickly developed their own character.

Other accounts of brewery visits have reported that the 6, 8, and 10 (with red, green, and blue caps respectively) are brewed from the same base, with the only difference the addition of dark sugar (and a little more hops for balance). That's not quite true. "They are members of the same team, with some variations," said Gumer Santos, Rochefort's brewing engineer. Rochefort uses the same Dingemans Pilsener and caramel malts throughout, with the gravity of the 8 and 10 boosted by grain as well as sugar.

"The process is the same, the recipe is not exactly the same," Santos said. "The more (gravity) you want, the more raw materials you need." A brew day produces 100 hectoliters (about 85 barrels) of 6 or 8 for the fermenter, while only 75 hectoliters of the 10 can be made. "If you change the (percentage of) malt too much, the yeast will not behave the same," Santos said.

All three beers exhibit many of the same flavor attributes, becoming more intense and showing their alcohol more as the numbers climb higher. Writing of *Rochefort 10*, Tim Webb offers one of the best beer descriptions ever penned: "A deep, dark, potent, warming cosmic meltdown of a forcefully contemplative brew, begging to be the last of the evening."

Brewery

Rochefort's brewhouse deserves the oft-repeated description "cathedral of beer." Other breweries might match the beauty of its traditional copper kettles, but the sight of colored rays created when sunlight passes through stained glass windows on its way to the shiny kettles reduces a visitor's voice to a church whisper. A copper lauter tun sits on a platform at one end, with a traditional mash-filter embedded in the tile wall. Only one of two kettles on the main level is used today; the other formerly collected second runnings to brew the refectory beer. Six monks participate in production, along with nine lay workers.

Rochefort takes its water from a spring, with the town drawing water from the same source. Water was a matter of pride even before De Clerck suggested cleaning up a nearby manure pile fifty years ago. "There are old papers in the archive that speak of its incredible purity," Santos said. While the stony hillsides of the Ardennes act as a natural filter, they also leave the water relatively hard, and higher in calcium and bicarbonate than at Chimay. The starting pH of 7 drops to 5.8–5.9 in the mash, with mineral acid used to reduce it to 5.2 in the kettle.

"Our water is irreplaceable," said Brother Pierre, who oversees brewing. "If you ask me, this makes the big difference between our beers and the Chimay beers. The water used in Chimay is much softer." The water difference might help explain why the yeast Father Theodore isolated for use at Chimay did not work as well at Rochefort. The brewery began using another in 1960, provided by the technical adviser at the time, who also worked at the Palm brewery. The yeast has three strains, two of which are very similar.

Brewers conduct a step-infusion mash, and Santos said he would rather not list details. Other visitors to the brewery report a 135-145-165-172° F (57-63-74-78° C) regimen. Rochefort includes a small amount of wheat starch in its beers. It previously added maize, but changed to wheat starch because of concerns about genetic modification. The starch primarily boosts alcohol content. "If you want to make a strong beer, you must do this. Otherwise, it would be too thick," Santos said.

Brewers add sugar in the kettle, both white and dark, as well as coriander with the last hop addition. Into the 1990s Rochefort took whole leaf hops and ground them up so the beer would be easier to centrifuge, but today it uses Styrian Goldings and Hallertau pellets.

Santos downplays the use of coriander. "It is a small amount, but people outside of Belgium think (Belgian brewers) use a lot of spices," he said. "Most of what they think are spices comes from the yeast."

Fermentation begins at 68° F (20° C), and the temperature rises to 73° F (23° C) during six to seven days of primary. In 2002 the brewery added cylindro-conical tanks, replacing closed fermentation vessels. Two have a capacity of 400 hecto-

A bobblehead from Saint Arnold Brewing Company in Texas sits beside bottles in the laboratory at Rochefort.

liters (340 barrels) and one 230, but workers only half-fill them. "People make a mistake when they produce a cigar tank, or rocket tank, that is three or four times taller than it is wide," Santos said. By filling the tanks halfway, Rochefort keeps the height (in this case 4 meters above the cone) and width (3.7 meters in diameter) about the same.

The new tanks were added when production expanded. "The father abbot is the only one who can choose (to raise production)," Santos said. "For many years we made 15,000 hectoliters a year. He decided that the community would be better off with a little increase in production. Now we will make up to 18,500 hectoliters (about 14,800 barrels). Instead of brewing three times a week, we will produce four times a week."

Rochefort 10

Original Gravity: 1.096 (23 °P)

Alcohol by Volume: 11.3%

Apparent Degree of Attenuation: 89%

IBU: 27

Malts: Pilsener, caramel

Adjuncts: White sugar, dark sugar, wheat starch

Spices: Coriander

Hops: Styrian Goldings, Hallertau

Yeast: Rochefort

Primary Fermentation: Yeast is pitched at 68° F (20° C), allowed to rise to 73° F (23° C), 7 days

Secondary Fermentation: 3 days at 46° F (8° C)

Also Noteworthy: Refermentation in the bottle with primary yeast

When the brewery starts a new yeast, it is used in the production of 6 for a week (four brews), then in the 8 for a week, and finally in the 10. The monks never reuse yeast from the 10.

Secondary fermentation lasts a rather short two or three days in horizontal lagering tanks, with yeast and sugar added after centrifuging. "We were taught in school to use 1 million cells per milliliter (for bottling), but to be safe I keep the count a little bit above that," Santos said. Rochefort aims for 7 grams (3.5 volumes) of CO_2 per liter in the bottle.

Beer spends ten days in a warm room at 73° F (23° C) before heading out the door. Brother Antoine, the monk responsible for the brewery from 1976 to 1997, probably put forth the idea that the 6 should be ready to drink after six weeks in the bottle, the 8 after eight, and the 10 after ten.

For years, bottle-conditioning took place in a long, well-fortified hallway directly under the church, and at the same time helped warm worshipers' feet. A variety of artifacts—such as large wooden barrels, a cart that was used to haul casks, and various bits of bottling equipment—now sit where bottles once conditioned.

On the day I visited, we came across a few cases of 10 from a bottling four days prior that had not gone to the warm room for conditioning. We opened a bottle, and there wasn't a hint of carbonation. At fifteen days since brewing began, the beer tasted of figs tossed in alcohol. Santos appeared pleased.

When fermentation doesn't go as well, isoamyl acetate esters pop above threshold levels, and banana notes such as those found in Chimay become more obvious. "(The fingerprint) should be a note of figs. Very complex, like figs with dried raisins, maybe anise," Santos said.

WESTMALLE

Were eighty new monks to join the monastery at Westmalle, it is doubtful any would take a job in the brewery. Not only would there be the matter of finding time for three brews a day and daily prayers, but as brewery manager Philippe Van Assche said, "Brewing takes special training and expertise that it didn't in the past."

While no monks remain as involved as Brother Thomas once was in Westmalle's brewing, they play an active role in the brewery operation. They sit on the board of administrators, hold all the shares of the separate brewing company, and control the investment and charitable decisions. "More and more, they try to give a large lump sum to bigger organizations," Van Assche said. "The same is true of the other abbeys. The trend is to consider it all together, to give a sum to the general abbot in Rome who will gather everything and divide it based on priorities worldwide."

According to those at other abbeys, Van Assche understates all that Westmalle contributes. As well as sending significant amounts of earnings to Rome, Westmalle lends financial aid to

Table 2.5 Westmalle Beers

Beer	Original Gravity SG (°Plato)	Alcohol (abv)	Apparent Degree of Attenuation	Color SRM (EBC)	IBU
Extra	1.046 (11.4 °P)	5.3%	88%	5 (10)	31
Dubbel	1.064 (15.6 °P)	7.3%	87%	37 (74)	24
Tripel	1.081 (19.6 °P)	9.6%	88%	6.5 (13)	39

Data provided by Derek Walsh; testing performed by De Proef Brouwerij. Color measured in EBC, converted to SRM by dividing by 1.97 (see p. 18).

several other struggling monasteries, and provides important brewing support to Westvleteren and Achel.

The board set three basic rules for the brewery:

- Production is capped at 120,000 hectoliters (about 102,000 barrels).
- There will be no changes in the recipe. "The only changes we know of are when some varieties (of ingredients) ceased to exist," Van Assche said.
- Advertising must be low profile. Westmalle has a solid presence in cafés and other beer establishments, including simple coasters and elegant leather menu binders.

Background

The monks who founded Westmalle fled France and first intended to escape to America. They occupied the monastery in the flatlands north and east of Antwerp beginning in 1802 and started brewing in 1836. The monks initially produced a

It takes just a minute to walk from Westmalle's quite modern plant through a tall passage that opens onto the nineteenth century monastery.

refectory beer for themselves and guests. They brewed a stronger beer for the first time in 1856, and sales at the gate began in 1860, shortly after a monk who had previous brewing experience joined the abbey. In 1865 the brewery expanded in order to help finance a Trappist abbey in the Congo.

Germans ransacked the brewery during World War I, and the monks began actively selling beer after rebuilding in 1920. Construction of a new brewery started in 1933, and it came on line in 1934. Westmalle consumed 400 tons of malt that year; today it uses 3,500 tons. The brewery complex, which encompasses a magnificent computerized bottling line installed in its midst in 2002, sits at one end of the monastery. A large portal opens from the brewery onto a view of late nineteenth century buildings, but it is easy for monks to go about their daily lives oblivious to the brewery, and for brewery visitors to come and go without seeing the monastery. Separate long lanes lead from the road to the brewery and monastery entrances. Stately elm trees line both lanes as well as the side of the abbey facing the nearby highway. Spent grain from brewing first feeds two hundred cattle on the abbey's surrounding farmland, and the rest goes to local farmers.

The community has twenty-five members, twenty of whom live within its walls. Brother Thomas, for instance, chose to live elsewhere after retiring.

Beers

Michael Jackson suggests that *Witkap Pater* may have been the first golden tripel, developed at the Drie Linden brewery. It certainly seems likely that Hendrik Verlinden was involved in developing a light-colored tripel, but it's not clear where.

Verlinden trained initially in distilling, published the first book in Flemish offering a scientific approach to yeast, and was a prominent consultant to breweries, distillers, and yeast producers. In the 1920s he aided the monks at Westmalle when problems arose with the *Dubbel Bruin*, and it would appear he continued a relationship after that. Verlinden, who had purchased the Drie Linden brewery in 1919, began producing beers in the Trappist style in 1929 and *Witkap Pater* (now known as *Witkap Tripel*) in 1932. While the monks at Westmalle and other Trappist breweries went to court to keep other secular brewers from labeling beer *Trappistenbier*, they allowed Verlinden to use the designation on his beers. Verlinden was killed in 1939 after a German bomb struck his brewery, and his family continued to use the *Trappistenbier* designation until 1981.

Westmalle Tripel

Original Gravity: 1.081 (19.6 °P)

Alcohol by Volume: 9.6%

Apparent Degree of Attenuation: 88%

IBU: 39

Malts: Pilsener

Adjuncts: Sugar (more than 15% of fermentables)

Hops: Tettnang, Saaz, Styrian Goldings, sometimes others

Yeast: Westmalle

Primary Fermentation: Yeast is pitched at 64° F (18° C), allowed to rise to 68° F (20° C), 5 to 6 days

Secondary Fermentation: 4 weeks at 46° F (8° C)

Also Noteworthy: Bottle-conditioned with primary yeast

Westmalle officially launched its *Tripel* when the new brewhouse debuted in 1934, but it appears experiments with a recipe began in 1931. Brother Thomas refined that recipe in the 1950s when he added more hops, and it has remained essentially unchanged since. Brother Thomas reworked the *Dubbel* at the same time, and that also has been brewed to the same specifications ever since. In 1980 *Dubbel* made up 70% of the brewery's sales; today *Tripel* accounts for 60% of sales.

The brewery produces a monks' beer, *Extra*, once or twice a year, calling it a "pils of high fermentation." The Belgians use the term "high fermentation" for ale, as opposed to "top fermented," and in the case of Trappist beers it properly hints of high attenuation. Brewed only with Pilsener malt (no sugar), *Extra* reaches an apparent attenuation of 88%, with its dry finish accented by a solid hop punch. Packaged without a label and 5.3% abv, *Extra* is reserved for the monks at Westmalle and Achel, but some bottles show up at beer festivals or otherwise sneak out of the brewery.

Brewery

At the entry to the brewhouse, bookshelves hold binders with years of brewing notes. Inside, a mash tun sits on one level, two 100-hectoliter (85-barrel) brewing kettles side by side on the other. A large white cross looms over the coppers. The brewery produces three 200-hectoliter batches per day, sometimes less on Fridays so that second-shift brewers can get home earlier.

Westmalle takes its water from a 70-meter- (230-foot-) deep well under the control of the local province. The brewery treats the water to reduce the iron, but otherwise the only adjustments are for pH in the kettle. Summer barley from

France is used to make the malts, produced to Westmalle's specifications by three maltsters. Brewers employ a step-infusion mash. The *Dubbel* includes a dark malt valued for its aroma, but Van Assche said dark sugar provides most of the color.

Westmalle uses only hop flowers in the kettle. At various times in the past, Brother Thomas reported including English Fuggles, Styrian Goldings, German Tettnang, Saaz, and a variety of others, keeping his hop recipes a secret. A recent visitor to the brewery spotted bags of Tettnang, Spalt Select, Saaz, and an unlabeled Russian hop.

The brewery buys sugar from several sources, adding it in liquid form at the end of a 90-minute boil. Sugar accounts for nearly 20% of the fermentables in the *Tripel*.

Westmalle Dubbel

Original Gravity: 1.063 (15.6 °P)

Alcohol by Volume: 7.3%

Apparent Degree of Attenuation: 87%

IBU: 24

Malts: Pilsener, caramel, dark malt for aroma

Adjuncts: Dark candi sugar (caramel syrup)

Hops: Tettnang, Styrian Goldings, Saaz

Yeast: Westmalle

Primary Fermentation: Yeast is pitched at 64° F (18° C), allowed to rise to 68° F (20° C), 5 to 6 days

Secondary Fermentation: 3 weeks at 46° F (8° C)

Also Noteworthy: Refermentation in the bottle with primary yeast

Westmalle converted to closed fermentation twenty years ago. "We were concerned, there's always a concern," Van Assche said. "They are very horizontal shaped, so the pressure column is very wide." Set behind tiled walls, the squarish 200-hectoliter (170-barrel) fermenters afford easy access for top cropping. One day in the winter of 2004-2005, a worker literally shoveled out yeast into stainless steel containers. The very modern Westmalle lab constantly checks the viability of the yeast, finding it necessary to start a new batch only once or twice a year.

While the lay worker, one of forty-one that the brewery employs, finished up, a young woman headed up the stairs toward the brewery, carrying a metal rack full of goblets brimming with brown-colored beer. Unlike the *Tripel* and *Extra*, a small amount of the *Dubbel* is refermented in the keg and available for draft dispense. Beer cafés take particular pride in being able to offer the draft *Dubbel*. Despite rumors that pop up on Internet message boards about *Westmalle Tripel* appearing as a draft product, inconsistent handling in the marketplace will keep the brewery from offering it on tap. Because the beers are only gently centrifuged, a certain amount of protein remains. While the darker *Westmalle Dubbel* hides chill haze and sediment from jostled kegs, the *Tripel* would lose much of its visual appeal.

Brewers pitch yeast at 64° F (18° C) and hold the fermenting wort to 68° F (20° C) during five to six days of primary. It lagers the *Dubbel* in horizontal tanks for three weeks, the *Tripel* for four weeks, then blends batches for consistency. Workers centrifuge the beer before bottling with the primary yeast (2 million cells per milliliter) and a dose of sugar. Westmalle aims for 6 to 8 grams (3 to 4 volumes) of CO_2 per liter in the bottle.

The warm room at Westmalle holds 125,000 cases of beer, which looks impressive until you realize it is less than one Anheuser-Busch plant produces in a single day.

The *Dubbel* takes two weeks to condition at 70 to 73° F (21 to 23° C), while the *Tripel* spends three weeks in carefully lit, temperature-controlled underground cellars that hold 125,000 cases.

WESTVLETEREN

The handwritten message across the top of the portal into the lower lagering cellar within the Westvleteren brewery simply reads: "SSST.... HIER RIJPT DE TRAPPIST," meaning "Quiet... here matures the Trappist." The words, inscribed by former brewer Brother Filip, mimic a much larger sign across a warehouse at the Moortgat Brewery, which admonishes drivers who speed by on the adjoining four-lane road not to disturb "den *Duvel.*"

The sign would be appropriate at the gates of the abbey Saint Sixtus of Westvleteren, except posting a banner wouldn't exactly suit the monks. Westvleteren tries to be the least commercial of the Trappist breweries, with the monks openly determined to remain involved in brewing without having it overshadow their daily lives. The monastery has the largest community of monks—twenty-eight—of the Trappists, and the youngest. The average age of 54 compares strikingly to the average of 76 within the religious community of surrounding West Flanders. The abbey makes a popular retreat, with the forty guest rooms always booked during Easter and often reaching capacity at other times. Guests may stay up to a week, joining in daily prayers. Some even volunteer for manual labor.

When the brewery modernized after World War I, introducing two new beers, Westvleteren looked to be on the same track as other monastery breweries. The abbey owned cafés that sold its beer, and after World War II easily could have chosen to expand. Instead, the abbot decided that too large a brewery would disturb the monastic spirit. As a result, Westvleteren sold all the cafés except the one across the road from the abbey, made a deal to have a Saint Sixtus beer brewed under license, and capped yearly production at 3,500 hectoliters (about 3,000 barrels).

A sign at the abbey tells what is for sale today, as does a recorded message on the beer phone (057-401057).

Westvleteren rescinded the contract-brewing deal after modernizing its own brewery in 1989, putting the monks back in control of all beer carrying the Saint Sixtus name. They sell that beer at the inn across the road and at the brewery gates. The beers have no labels; the crowns carry all the required legal information. When customers buy beer at the abbey, the receipt states that the beer cannot be resold. Café owners within Belgium have long been able to acquire limited quantities, usually reselling it for a price not too much more than other Trappist beers. Some owners decorate the bar area with empty wooden crates carrying the Westvleteren stamp.

The monks have no interest in selling their beer through distributors. That an American importer acquired their beer through third parties in the late 1990s, added labels to the bottles, and sold it in the United States runs counter to their monastic ethic. "We do not advertise, we have no publicity," said Brother Joris, the monk in charge of brewing. "We live on brewing, but we do it so we can continue with our real business, which is being monks."

Where possible, the monks have gone through legal authorities to choke off sales in the United States. "If we had a label, it would say, 'Do not import to the United States,' " said Brother Joris.

Background

The abbey blends into the pastoral countryside only minutes north of Poperinge, the center of hop growing in Belgium, and just across the border from France. Three different monasteries, attracting at different times monks or nuns, operated in the region between 806 and 1784. The land lay bare when Jan-Baptist Victoor left Poperinge in 1814 to settle in the woods of Saint Sixtus, live as a hermit, and take up the monastic tradition wiped out in 1790. In the summer of 1831, just a year after Belgium asserted its independence from the Netherlands, a few monks from the nearby monastery of Mont de Cats joined the hermit to start the new Trappist monastery.

Table 2.6 Westvleteren Beers

Beer	Original Gravity SG (°Plato)	Alcohol (abv)	Apparent Degree of Attenuation	Color SRM (EBC)	IBU
Westvleteren Blond	1.051 (12.6 °P)	5.6%	84%	4.5 (9)	41
Westvleteren 8	1.072 (17.6 °P)	8.3%	88%	36 (72)	35
Westvleteren 12	1.090 (21.5 °P)	10.2%	86%	40 (79)	38

Data provided by Derek Walsh; testing performed by De Proef Brouwerij. Color measured in EBC, converted to SRM by dividing by 1.97 (see p. 18).

Brewing began in 1839 a copy of the license from King Leopold sits on display in the Claustrum—with sales out the door beginning in 1871. Monastery records show that modernization and brewery expansion continued into the twentieth century. To fund construction of a new abbey in 1928, the brewery expanded, both in capacity and the range of beers offered. Jackson's *Great Beers of Belgium* shows sepia-toned photos of Westvleteren's monks bottling beer or serving it to the public during this era.

Westvleteren didn't neglect brewing during the period it licensed the use of the Saint Sixtus name. When customers at the inn and drive-up complained about the quality of the beer, Brother Thomas from Westmalle—rather than an outside brewing engineer—offered advice. In 1968 the brewery replaced wooden fermentation tanks with stainless steel. In 1989 Westvleteren totally overhauled the brewhouse, installing a modern stainless steel showcase, replacing a mash tun covered with wood and brewing kettles that were bricked-in vessels with copper lids.

Beers

Until 1999, when Brother Filip created the new *Westvleteren Blond* to mark the opening of the remodeled *In de Vrede* café, the beers could be called simply *4, 6, 8,* and *12* and identified by the color of their caps—green, red, blue, and yellow, respectively. At different times, they were known as *Dubbel, Special, Extra,* and *Abt,* respectively. All but the *4* were dark. The new *Blond* replaced both the *4* and *6,* and the monks may drink it with their lunch. The *Blond* packs a hop punch worthy of being brewed within sight of hop poles, although it doesn't get the attention of the powerful *8* (8.3% abv) and *12* (10.3% abv).

Records indicate the *Westvleteren 12* has evolved since first being introduced in the 1930s, when it actually started at 12 degrees Belgian (1.120) and was 12% abv. That beer finished at 1.029 (7.3 °P), for apparent attenuation of 76%. Records indicate lower attenuation at other times, with a final gravity as high at 1.039 (9.8 °P). Today the beer reaches 86% apparent attenuation, finishing at 1.013 (3.4 °P).

Brewery

The new brewhouse, remodeled to look like the original brewery on the outside, replaced the former malt barn. Whitewashed brick walls create a farmhouse feel on the agrarian end of the monastery. Arched windows afford a spacious view of the flat, surrounding farmland. The monks no longer farm, leasing the land to local farmers who must grow only crops such as winter corn and potatoes, so as not to obstruct the monks' view.

The rhythm of monastic life remains intact in the brewery. The monks brew seventy times a year—twenty-five to twenty-six weeks and two to three days per week—producing 4,750 hecto-liters (about 4,050 barrels). They brew one week and bottle the next, adding yeast taken from a high kräusen of an ongoing fermentation. On brewing days, a secular worker drives to Westmalle to pick up the yeast for primary fermentation. We don't know when Westvleteren quit using its own yeast, which might live on in an altered condition at Saint Bernardus (where

Westvleteren 8

Original Gravity: 1.072 (17.6 °P)

Alcohol by Volume: 8.3%

Apparent Degree of Attenuation: 88%

IBU: 35

Malts: Pale, Pilsener

Adjuncts: Sucrose, caramelized sugar

Hops: Northern Brewer, Hallertau, Styrian Goldings

Yeast: Westmalle

Primary Fermentation: Yeast is pitched at 68° F (20° C), rises to 82 to 84° F (28 to 29° C), 4 to 6 days

Secondary Fermentation: 4 to 6 weeks at 50° F (10° C)

Also Noteworthy: Refermentation in the bottle with yeast cropped from primary fermentation

Saint Sixtus was contract brewed), since the brewing connection to Westmalle and Brother Thomas goes back to the 1960s. Others have reported that Westvleteren may have once used yeast from Rodenbach.

Brother Joris took over the job of running the brewery from Brother Filip in mid-2004. From 1995 to 1999 Brother Joris operated the fermentation room and did the laboratory work, then focused on liturgical matters. He still operates the monastery library and also deals with accounting matters. Brother Jos supervises brewhouse operations, and another monk does the lab work.

"We check each step, we do the controls," Brother Joris said. "If there is a problem, then we take it to Westmalle."

One monk runs sales at the gate, and another aids him. Three laymen work in the brewery and do other jobs at the monastery when they aren't brewing. Bottling occupies seven monks and the three lay workers.

The water of the surrounding area is harder than at other Trappist breweries, and particularly higher in bicarbonate, chloride, and sulfate. "It is treated," Brother Joris said. "That is part of the brewery's secret." The brewery uses only two malts, Dingemans pale and Pilsener, in all its beers. The proportion of the two remains the same in all three beers, with plain sugar added to each. Westvleteren uses three hops from the Poperinge area, with extracts at the start of the boil for bittering and pellets for flavor. Jackson has reported Northern Brewer is used for bittering, and others have listed the use of Styrian Goldings and Hallertau for flavor.

Brother Jos says only that the boil lasts at least sixty minutes to isomerize the hop alpha acids. When he brews the *8* and *12* at the same time (the *12* comprises about 50% of production, the *8* 35%), the bulk of the high-gravity runnings go to the 34-hectoliter (29-barrel) kettle with the *12*. The monks won't reveal how the dark beers obtain their color, as well as the intriguing flavors traditionally produced by darker malts and/or dark sugar. However, Jackson and others report the use of caramelized sugar. A longer boil also adds color.

Westvleteren is the last Trappist brewery to still ferment in open vessels, with two 68-hectoliter squares and four of 34 hectoliters. After the boil ends and the wort chills, one monk waits in the fermentation room with a hose. When he hears a horn blow, he points the hose into a fermenter and waits for beer to arrive. Fermentation begins at 68° F (20° C) and rises to 82 to 84° F (28 to 29° C). "At least 28, even in winter," Brother Joris said. Because the temperature of the fermentation room varies by season, he must restrain the temperature using only water that flows through the walls of the fermenters. Sometimes he'll visit the brewery in the middle of the night, because if the yeast gets too hot, and he tries to rein it in, it is prone to crashing.

After apparent attenuation reaches 76 to 80%, he begins cooling the beer to 68° F (20° C). In a typical week, the monks brew *Blond* on Monday and Tuesday, and by Friday it can be moved to lagering tanks, where it will remain at 50° F (10° C) for four weeks. The dark beers spend four to six days in primary before lagering. Because Westvleteren neither filters nor centrifuges, yeast, hops, and proteins must settle out naturally (about 8% of volume is lost in the process). "The length depends on the speed of becoming clear," said Brother Joris. The *8* usually takes at least a month, and the *12* might take two months to ten weeks, "when you get a difficult one."

The brewhouse at Westvleteren is modern, but the bottling line is not.

As at other breweries, Westvleteren sells spent grain to local farmers. Some of the yeast left in horizontal lagering tanks is fed to livestock, some sent to the nearby French Abbaye de Belval, where monks use it wash cheese. "Very monastic," Brother Joris said of the recycling process. *In De Vrede* sells the cheese.

Monks add sugar and yeast to a 130-hectoliter (110-barrel) bottling tank after the beer clarifies enough to bottle. Although they use the bottling line installed in 1979 only thirty-five to thirty-six days a year, it doesn't look like it could survive many more years. "I'm always relieved when the beer is in the bottle," Brother Joris said.

The *Blond* spends eight days at 79° F (26° C) to bottle-condition, while the *8* and *12* take ten and twelve days, respectively.

SSST…. HIER RIJPT DE TRAPPIST.

three

Beyond the
Heavenly Gates

W hen we trace the history of beers considered Trappist-like, one path doesn't lead back to a monastery. Instead, we stop in the town of Breendonk, where the Moortgat family brewery created a beer whose name sounds very much like the Flemish for "devil." The brewery merits a visit not only because strong golden ale originated there, but because it produces beer with Cistercian patience.

Like the Trappists, the fortunes of the Moortgat brewery rose with growing demand for strong beer following World War I and the prohibition on spirits. And like the Trappists, it owes a debt to brewing scientist Jean De Clerck.

Duvel once was a darker beer. The story goes that a brewery worker who had a test batch called it "The devil of a beer," and so it took its name from the Flemish word for devil, *duivel*. After lighter-colored Pilseners grew in popularity, Moortgat, like nearby Westmalle (though nearly forty years later), decided to brew a strong, lighter-colored beer—and did it by reformulating its own *Duvel* in 1970. De Clerck helped, using a very light Pilsener malt made at the brewery's own maltings, which

Photo courtesy Derek Walsh.

operated into the 1980s. *Duvel's* paler color became a trade-mark, and at 3-4 SRM (7 EBC) it is considerably lighter than *Westmalle Tripel* at 6-7 SRM (13 EBC).

The thoroughly modern brewery in Breendonk produces a wide range of beers, from Pilseners to the Maredsous abbey beers, but *Duvel* accounts for 85% of output, explaining why the brewery established in 1871 was renamed Duvel Moortgat in the 1990s. The Moortgats were original investors in Brewery Ommegang in New York, and implemented full-scale expansion after buying full control of the brewery in 2003.

Standing in front of a control panel, where a worker can change the temperature within the fermentation cylinder with one touch and set the temperature of the cone with another, technical director Hedwig Neven described how each process within the fermentation area can be controlled from this spot. "Every valve, every connection can be cleaned," he said. Then he explained the yeast recuperation system, where

Duvel

Original Gravity: 1.069 (16.9 °P)

Alcohol by Volume: 8.4%

Apparent Degree of Attenuation: 93%

IBU: 30

Malts: Pilsener (blend of varieties)

Adjuncts: Dextrose (about 17% of fermentables)

Hops: Stryian Goldings, Saaz

Yeast: Duvel

Primary Fermentation: Yeast pitched at 61 to 64° F (16 to 18° C), rises to 79 to 84° F (26 to 29° C), 120 hours

Secondary Fermentation: Cooled to 27° F (-3° C), held below 32° F (0° C) for 3 weeks

Also Noteworthy: Refermentation in the bottle

slight overpressure in the tank forces the top-cropping yeast up through a tube on one side, allowing the brewery to top crop from a conical even more effectively than from a square or an open fermenter. "This doesn't exist anywhere else in the world," Neven said.

Brewery employees monitor each step of the brewing process with unusual care. "When you don't measure (at any point), then you won't be able to proceed to the next step. Total production will stop, and you will be sending water to the bottling line," he said. "Production is a slave of quality control. This is a system we developed ourselves. We are more quality driven than efficiency driven."

Duvel long has been known for the meticulous manner in which it conditions, referments, and continues to condition its beer. After primary fermentation, beer lagers for three weeks below freezing. Filled at 68° F (20° C), bottles spend ten days to two weeks undergoing refermentation at 75° F (24° C) in a warm room heated from both the floor and ceiling. The beer then rests six weeks at 41° F (5 to 6° C) before being released. Endless rows of cases of *Duvel*, stacked to the ceiling, all in various stages of maturation, fill large warehouses. A large sign painted on the side of one reads, "Ssst ... hier rijpt den *Duvel*," meaning the beer is ripening (or maturing).

Some customers further cellar the beer for several months. "We want the evolution to take place at home," Neven said. "Our goal is to sell our beer as fresh as possible."

The regimen existed well before Neven joined Moortgat in 1997, but it hardly seems coincidental that when he received his doctorate from the Catholic University of Leuven, he presented a paper on the evolution of aromatic elements in beer during bottle-conditioning.

"We'll always maintain the old recipes while developing (our equipment) for the latest (brewing) techniques," he said on a day late in 2004. He described planned renovations, including a new brewhouse and water treatment plant, and talked about innovative equipment that would be installed. "We will look at the newest techniques and choose the ones that are best for our beer products. You try to optimize the process," he said. Only the recipe can't change. "It's not the recipe (for *Duvel*) of the brewer who came before me, either. The challenge is in optimizing everything that's around the recipe."

Moortgat takes water, quite soft and free of iron, from four wells, each 60 meters (almost 200 feet) deep. Brewers add necessary salts after de-mineralization. Warehouses replaced malting facilities in the 1980s, so the brewery relies on four different malt suppliers, two from Belgium and two from France. The brewery uses only Pilsener malts in *Duvel*, blending varieties made from French barley. Moortgat maintains hop contracts seven years into the future, using Styrian Goldings and Saaz hops in pellet form from Slovenia and the Czech Republic. Three different suppliers provide dextrose sugar.

The yeast was taken from a culture out of a bottle-conditioned *McEwan's Scotch Ale* after World War I. The culture had between ten and twenty strains, and De Clerck "took them apart" to isolate one. Neven said the brewers use a single strain today—for the Maredsous beers as well as *Duvel*—but that "circumstances for the strain are different when used for bottle-conditioning."

The brewery employs a traditional step mash for all its beers and boils *Duvel* for ninety minutes, adding dextrose in the kettle. Bittering hops are added twenty-five minutes into the boil, about two-thirds of mass, and aroma hops at sixty minutes. The brewery produces thirty-six 230-hectoliter (195-barrel) batches of *Duvel* a week. Four brews fill 1,000-hectoliter (850-barrel) tanks for primary fermentation, then batches are blended

Photo courtesy Derek Walsh.

into one of fifteen 2,000-hectoliter tanks for secondary. Primary fermentation lasts 120 hours, with the temperature adjusted to assure it remains on schedule. Fermentation begins at 61 to 64° F (16 to 18° C), depending on how many generations the yeast has been used, and tops out at between 77 and 84° F (25 to 29° C). Yeast will be cropped during high kraeusen, at about 72° F (22° C).

"When the new tanks were installed, we were very concerned about the ester profile," Neven said. He was delighted to find that the concentration of isoamyl acetate (banana and fruit character) dropped from about 3 to 4 milligrams per liter to 2 to 3 milligrams per liter. "We now have a more controllable attenuation, when means more controllable refermentation," he said.

Maredsous 8

Original Gravity: 1.069 (16.9 °P)

Alcohol by Volume: 8.1%

Apparent Degree of Attenuation: 83%

IBU: 29

Malts: Pilsener, caramalt, roasted malt

Adjuncts: Dextrose

Hops: Styrian Goldings, Saaz

Yeast: Duvel

Primary Fermentation: Yeast pitched at 61 to 64° F (16 to 18° C), rises to 79 to 84° F (26 to 29° C), 5 days

Secondary Fermentation: 2 weeks at 46° F (8° C)

Also Noteworthy: Refermentation in the bottle with primary yeast

Moortgat doses beer with sugar and 1 million cells per milliliter of fresh yeast, compared to 3 to 4 million ten years ago, for bottling. *Duvel* contains 4 to 5 grams of CO_2 per liter before bottle-conditioning, 8.5 grams per liter (which equates to 4.25 volumes) after refermentation. The beer pours with a spectacular white head that tries your patience if you decide to wait for it to dissipate.

Moortgat has brewed Maredsous abbey beers under contract since 1963. The *Maredsous 6* and *Maredsous 10* include caramel malts on top of a Pilsener base, while the *Maredsous 8* contains caramel and roasted malt. Like *Duvel* all three beers are brewed with dextrose and fermented with Duvel yeast. "That adds drinkability," Neven said. "You don't want beers that are too sweet or too abundant or too spicy. Those are not digestible."

Duvel finishes extraordinarily dry, with apparent attenuation above 90%, setting itself apart from a long list of competitors who have devilish names but can't seem to help being sweet. Beer writer Michael Jackson dubbed it a strong golden ale when he was handing out style names, while American homebrewers call it golden strong, and competitors in professional competitions a pale strong ale. They know they are all talking about the same beer—*Duvel*.

"It's not only a brand name, but a type name," Neven said.

four
Abbey Ales

The term abbey ale represents neither a single style nor a family of beers, but Belgian beer consumers associate "abbey" on a label with the same range of strong beers that Trappists produce. Their presence in the marketplace cannot be overlooked. In 2003 abbey beers outsold Trappist beers more than 2.5 to 1 in Belgium and more than 8 to 1 elsewhere. No wonder abbeys that no longer brew, or maybe never brewed, happily license their name to secular breweries, or that secular breweries seek out deals to produce beers they may call abbey.

Unlike the Trappist mark that assures a beer was brewed inside a monastery, the Certified Belgian Abbey beer logo guarantees nothing about where the beer might be produced. In some cases the commercial brewery—Saint Feuillien, for instance—could be a relatively small independent. In other cases the controlling commercial brewing company represents one of the biggest in the world.

This chapter examines beers that carry the certified mark, plus others with a strong abbey connection. In the next chapter, we visit many independent breweries, some of which also make an abbey connection.

Abbey ale producers lean heavily on marketing the monastic brewing tradition. In his book *Blink*, Malcolm Gladwell writes, "When we put something in our mouth, and in that blink of an eye decide whether it tastes good or not, we are reacting not only to the evidence from our taste buds and salivary glands but also to the evidence of our eyes and memories and imaginations."[1]

The association between drinking a glass of *Orval*, looking at a picture of the ruins of Abbaye d'Orval, and fondly remembering a visit to the abbey should not be underestimated. Those who sell abbey beers  hope to tap into the same monastic connection. That's one reason why visitors to the Affligem website (*www.affligembeer.be*) hear monks chanting in the background.

To the Belgian beer drinker, the terms Trappist and abbey indicate the same sort of beer. "There is no Trappist style," said Carl Kins, who traveled from Belgian to judge at the 2004 Great American Beer Festival. "For abbey-style-type of beers I tasted and judged, overall, the style has gotten smoother and/or sweet. Actually, most breweries try to follow the market leader (Leffe) and make a beer that has less character so as to appeal to a larger market."

THE MULTINATIONALS

InBev and Heineken, two of the world's largest brewing companies, control two of the best-known abbey brands, boosting their international exposure. For instance, at the same time that Belgium-based InBev (then known as Interbrew) rolled out *Stella Artois* in New York City, it invested in a Belgian-style

[1] Gladwell, *Blink: The Power of Thinking Without Thinking* (New York: Little, Brown, 2005), 165.

Official Abbey Beers

The Belgian Brewers, a trade organization, authorizes the use of a Certified Belgian Abbey beer logo. Qualified abbey beers must:

- Have a link with an existing abbey or a former abbey.
- Pay royalties for charities or to protect the cultural heritage of the abbey, or to benefit an institution that represents a former abbey.
- The abbey or existing institution has control over advertising material.

Which beers qualify, and where they are brewed, changes often.

Brand	Brewery (owner)
Affligem	Affligem (Heineken)
Bonne Esperance	Lefebvre
Bornem	Van Steenberge
Cambron	Silly
Dendernonde	Block
Ename	Roman
Floreffe	Lefebvre
Grimbergen	Union (S&N Alken-Maes)
Konigshoeven	Konigshoeven (Bavaria)
Leffe	Hoegaarden/Artois (InBev)
Maredsous	Moortgat
Postel	Affligem (Heineken)
St Feuillien	St Feuillien
Steenbrugge	Palm
Tongerlo	Haacht
Val-Dieu	Val-Dieu

restaurant in what was once the meatpacking district of Manhattan. Markt, serving other Belgian beers but advertising Leffe on a large rooftop sign, soon became the center of an area *The New York Times* dubbed "Little Belgium." Just as impressively, Affligem sales more than tripled in the first three years after Heineken bought full interest in the brewery.

Leffe

Notre-Dame de Leffe was one of the first monasteries to enter a formal licensing arrangement with a commercial brewery, beginning in 1952. Leffe beers became well known worldwide because the small brewery that struck the deal with the abbey was taken over by another brewing company, and that one by another, and eventually the brewing giant InBev, still known as Interbrew in Belgium, owned the brand. The Leffe logo picturing an abbey set in stained glass appears *everywhere* in Belgium.

Some advertising for Leffe implies that the current recipes are preserved from a time the abbey made its own beer. Norbertine monks founded the abbey in 1152 on the River Meuse, about 50 miles southwest of Brussels. They almost surely brewed shortly thereafter, but not continuously, since the abbey

Leffe Blond

Original Gravity: 1.064 (15.6 °P)

Alcohol by Volume: 6.6%

Apparent Degree of Attenuation: 81%

IBU: 25

Malts: Pilsener, pale malt

Adjuncts: Maize

Hops: Hallertau, Saaz

Yeast: House yeast

Primary Fermentation: Yeast pitched at 64° F (18° C), rises to 77° F (25° C), 4 to 5 days

Secondary Fermentation: 30° F (-1° C) for 2 weeks

Also Noteworthy: No refermentation in the bottle

itself was sacked in the fifteenth century. In the seventeenth century the monks employed a layman to do the brewing, and records indicate that he died a rich man. By the early eighteenth century the brewery expanded, providing funds to build a new church. After being ravaged in 1794, the abbey became national property and was split up and sold in parts. Two former abbots of Leffe briefly tried to maintain the surrounding hop fields and brewery, but brewing ended by 1809.

Most of the monastery's buildings date to the seventeenth and eighteenth centuries, although they were sold in 1816 and transformed into workshops. When the French chased out the Norbertines of Saint Michel de Frigolet, the monks took refuge in Belgium in 1902, buying many of the old buildings and reviving the abbey.

Interbrew produces the Leffe beers at its high-tech Artois brewery in Leuven. Leffe, a short drive from the Abbey of Maredsous and the Floreffe Abbey, maintains a museum with an interactive exhibit.

Affligem

Located on the border between Flemish Brabant and East Flanders, the Affligem abbey has a history as rich as Leffe's, and its beers might be as well known in the United States. Six pillaging knights who became Benedictines built the abbey in 1074. Artifacts indicate the abbey brewed beer for pilgrims as early as 1129, and it has many important links to hop trading. Hops still grow on hillsides below the monastery. Its buildings were laid to waste several times over the centuries, but the monks rebuilt each time. Until the French Revolution, they employed layman to make beer, then did their own brewing into the twentieth century.

Affligem Blonde

Original Gravity: 1.065 (16 °P)

Alcohol by Volume: 6.8%

Apparent Degree of Attenuation: 80%

IBU: 24

Malts: Pilsener, Munich

Hops: Hallertau, Spalt, Styrian Goldings

Yeast: Affligem

Primary Fermentation: 5 days

Secondary Fermentation: 14 days

Also Noteworthy: Bottle-conditioned

Affligem rebuilt its brewery after the Germans destroyed it in World War I, but when it was ransacked again during World War II, they struck a deal to have the beer made at De Hertog. Production moved to nearby Opwijk in the 1970s, first under contract with the De Smedt brewery, which later changed its name to Affligem and then was sold to Heineken. When the brewery was still known as De Smedt, visitors were told that the recipes were the same as those used for the beers tasted by Godefroid de Bouillon in 1096 and Saint Bernard in 1146 on their respective visits to Affligem. Today Affligem advertises beer brewed to an original recipe that was refined by a monk named Tobias in the twentieth century to take advantage of modern techniques. He called the result "Formula Antiqua Renovata."

After being taken over by Heineken, Affligem sales grew from 50,000 hectoliters (42,600 barrels) in 1999 to 160,000 (136,300 barrels) in 2003. The abbey continues to own the brand name and a guarantee that the beer must continue to be brewed in Belgium for the next thirty years. Like the Trappists, Affligem uses proceeds from beer sales for charitable purposes, including a recently created youth farm.

SOMETIMES AN ABBEY, SOMETIMES NOT

For a brief period in 1999 there were seven sanctioned Trappist breweries. The monks at Schaapskooi in the Netherlands

Just outside of Affligem, a sign at the abbey reminds potential worshipers about services.

lost the right to label their beers as an "Authentic Trappist Product" after selling control to Dutch brewing giant Bavaria, a company whose flagship *Bavaria* beer sells in eighty-two countries worldwide.

Bavaria continues to market *La Trappe/Konigshoeven* as Trappist beer, and in 2005 the monastery applied to again use the Trappist mark. Although beers from Schaapskooi carry the *Konigshoeven* label in the United States, they are still better known here as *La Trappe*. Even before Bavaria took control of the brand, the brewery aggressively marketed *La Trappe*, including taking out full-page advertisements in magazines.

"Our Belgian colleagues think we are too commercial. But what can you do?" brewery manager Peter Peters said in 1999. "The future for Trappists is far from rosy! The number of monks is falling constantly, and we do not have any monks at

Table 4.1- La Trappe Beers

Beer	Original Gravity SG (°Plato)	Alcohol (abv)	Apparent Degree of Attenuation	Color SRM (EBC)	IBU
Blond	1.061 (14.9 °P)	6.7%	84%	9 (18)	14
Dubbel	1.066 (16.2 °P)	7%	80%	48 (95)	12
Tripel	1.076 (18.5 °P)	8.3%	81%	20 (40)	14
Quadrupel	1.086 (20.8 °P)	9.5%	81%	28 (56)	18

Data provided by Derek Walsh; testing performed by De Proef Brouwerij and Westmalle. Color measured in EBC, converted to SRM by dividing by 1.97 (see p. 18).

all working in our brewery right now. This is why from 1999 we have joined forces with Bavaria. The monastery simply cannot continue to support the brewery, and distribution has always been our big problem. Bavaria can help us there."[2]

Here are seven more heavenly relationships:

Corsendonk: The former Corsendonk Priory closed in 1784, and its buildings were restored in the 1970s as a conference center. Corsendonk beers, created in 1982, don't carry the certified abbey stamp, although their bottles are ornately decorated with a seal that dates to the fifteenth century. The tripel, sold as *Abbey Pale Ale* in the United States, goes by the name of *Agnus* in Belgium. *Abbey Brown Ale*, called *Pater Noster* in Belgium, has long been available in the United States and introduced many Americans to the darker abbey profile.

Grimbergen and Ciney: Alken-Maes, now owned by global brewing power Scottish & Newcastle, has produced Grimbergen since 1954 at its Union brewery, an old-style plant with a distinctly industrial feel. Grimbergen labels

---

[2] Filip Verheyden. "Trappist Beers from La Trappe." *Bier Passion* 5 (December/January/February 2001), 10.

feature a phoenix on stained glass with the inscription "Ardet Nec Consumitur" ("Burnt but Never Destroyed"), celebrating the fact that the Norbertine monastery was successfully rebuilt four times. The brewery claims to have preserved the secret of the first Grimbergen beers, if not the actual recipes. Alken-Maes also brews Ciney beers at its Union plant. Named after a small town near France, Ciney beers are fermented with different yeast than Grimbergen but have the same sweet stamp as Grimbergen. The abbey tower image on Ciney bottles prominently decorates signs outside company-related beer cafés, implying a strong church connection, although no link with any abbey exists.

St Feuillien Tripel

Original Gravity: 1.074 (18 °P)

Alcohol by Volume: 8.5%

Apparent Degree of Attenuation: 86%

IBU: 28

Malts: Pilsener, CaraPils

Adjuncts: Sugar

Hops: Styrian Goldings, Spalt, Saaz

Yeast: Not specified, brewed in 2 locations

Primary Fermentation: Yeast pitched at 68° F (20° C), rises to 73° F (23° C), 7 days

Secondary Fermentation: 6 weeks at 32° F (0° C)

Also Noteworthy: Refermentation in the bottle

Saint Feuillien: About thirty to forty monks once inhabited the Abbey of Saint Feuillien, founded in Le Roeulx from 1125 and occupied until the French sacked it in  1790. In 1873 Stephanie Friart founded a brewery in Le Roeulx that operated until it closed in 1977. The Friart family revived the brewery in 1988. Saint Feuillien produces beer for large bottles on site and contracts out production of beer sold in 330ml and 750ml bottles to Brasserie du Bocq. Saint Feuillien regularly sells bottles of up to 9 liters (called Salmanazars) and occasionally fills even bigger ones. Its beers undergo a particularly long, cold secondary, spending six weeks at 0° C (32° F) and then three weeks bottle-conditioning.

Tongerlo: The Norbertine abbey of Tongerlo lords magnificently over flat lands just south of the Netherlands, licensing production to the Haacht brewery. Although 90% of the beer it makes is Pilsener, Haacht affords Tongerlo a solid presence in many city centers because it promotes the abbey connection prominently in its 5,000 beer cafés (most called Primus).

Val-Dieu: Brewing returned to the abbey grounds in 1996, in former farm buildings amid a collection of well-kept seventeenth- and eighteenth-century structures, making this the only non-Trappist monastery in Belgium where beer is produced. However, no monks brew; in fact, none live at Val-Dieu. Christian families, who offer the grounds as a place for retreat, manage the complex. Cistercians established the Val-Dieu abbey in 1216 and brewed once upon a time. The brewery says recipes for the current Val-Dieu beers were passed on by the last of the monastery's abbots before his death.

Witkap: Brouwerij Slaghmuylder has operated its family brewery in East Flanders for more than one hundred and fifty years, these days producing both lagers and distinctive Witkap beers that include an outstanding tripel. Witkap refers to the white cowls of Cistercians monks, and Drie Linden brewed the range of beers until 1981. Because Hendrik Verlinden of Drie Linden helped Westmalle with brewing matters in the 1920s and probably assisted in formulating its *Tripel*, the monks let Witkap beers carry the *Trappistenbier* designation. *Witkap Stimulo*, a 6% beer similar to (although a bit stronger than) beers made only for the monks in Trappist breweries, goes by the name of *Witkap Pater* in the United States.

five

Independent Spirits

When Michael Jackson visited Chimay and La Trappe in the late 1980s for his *Beer Hunter* television series, he also talked to principals at three small Dutch breweries about why they attempted to produce beers that emulated the Trappists (La Trappe was at the time a certified Trappist brewery). They didn't discuss the commercial appeal of selling abbey beers, but the beers themselves and why they wanted to brew them.

"Although I'm not very religious, what those monks makes is very tasty," said Kaspar Peterson, who founded Brouwerij 't Ij with money he earned from writing hit rock songs. "I try to make beer that is more or less like those." He gave them something other than monastic names, calling the dubbel *Natte* ("wet") and the tripel *Zatte* ("drunk").

Herm Hegger described making the beers for his Raaf brewery as a rite of passage, much like American microbrewers in the 1990s might have spoken of mastering hoppy beers. "It is a good thing to show you can make a good dubbel and tripel. They are difficult to make," he said. "For me, it was also a way to show I'm a professional brewer. I became a professional when I was working on them."

This chapter focuses on two breweries making distinctive beers related to Trappist products in much the same way Trappist beers are connected to each other. That is, they brew beers of "high fermentation"—well-attenuated, "digestible," and bottle-conditioned. We'll also peek inside five more independent breweries making similar beers. They may produce beers called dubbel and tripel, and they may not, choosing those names not so much to imply association with an abbey but because they tell consumers what kind of beer to expect.

Trappist breweries promote the idea that their recipes no longer change, marketing quality and consistency. Monks, once the innovators, have left the field open to independents on both sides of the Atlantic.

Some of the breweries look about as modern as the sepia-toned photos from Westvleteren featured in Jackson's *Great Beers of Belgium*. Others operate on the cutting edge of technology, such as the De Proef Brouwerij in West Flanders, which produces not only its own beers but scores of private labels. "We want to show our customers that the craft of brewing is as important today as it ever was," said founder Dirk Naudts. "Brewing with the necessary craftsmanship, following the rules of the art. Artisanal is not a synonym for dirty or old-fashioned; it means brewing as one ought to, while at the same time applying modern know-how and technology."

A monk could not have said it better.

BROUWERIJ KERKOM

If Disney were to add a farmhouse brewery to one of its theme parks, it would be wise to simply buy this one in the Limburg countryside south of Saint Truden and reinstall it as is. "The

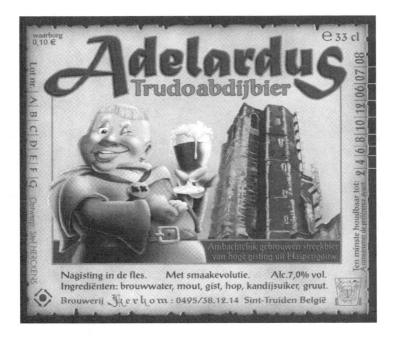

first time I saw this place, I knew I had to brew here," said owner Marc Limet, looking around the cobblestone courtyard. Whitewashed brick walls surround the courtyard, with artifacts from the past century scattered about. These include delivery wagons packed with bottles and wooden barrels as well as hundreds of other colorful bottles in painted crates.

The small café area has two small bars side by side, one with a marble top and the other with a well-aged counter top, and proper glassware for each of the Bink beers (the brewery's name brand) stand in ready behind. The interior matches the courtyard for character and comfort, with old photos and advertisements for current community events decorating the walls and unmatched chairs sitting haphazardly at wooden tables.

What the menu at the the café at Brouwerij Kerkom lacks in quantity it makes up for in quality.

Not surprisingly, brewers send other brewers to drink here. Visitors sometimes include brewing engineers trained to work in large modern breweries. They receive a history lesson when they step into what might be called the south wing, which has been home to a brewery off and on since 1878. It's easy to imagine when hay would have been stored in the loft, with animals housed there. The mill looks as if it was new not long after the brewery opened, while brick encloses the mash kettle. "You cannot brew beer with less equipment," Limet said.

Limet continued his story as we visited various cafés that serve his beer. "Those brewing engineers cannot believe it is possible to make beer on that system," he said. By now we were eating a three-course afternoon meal at *Het Vijgeblad* in Beringen, north of Hasselt, each dish prepared with one of Limet's beers. He brews two different private labels for the café during the year. On a Sunday, owner-chef Philip

Reynders found time to wait on our table, seemingly making up the dishes as he went.

Limet continued with his story. "I tell them I am just a brewer," he said.

Reynders arrived as if it were rehearsed. "He's a brewer, not an Interbrewer," he said, referring to the brewing giant known as InBev worldwide but Interbrew in Belgium, and making it clear whose beer he preferred.

Kerkom produced a modest 600 hectoliters (less than 500 barrels) in 2004, brewing four to six times a month, blending batches from the 14-hectoliter system into one of three 30-hectoliter tanks or one of five 10-hectoliter tanks. Limet rushes nothing, letting primary fermentation last ten days. "For ten days I do nothing. I let the beer rest," he said.

Limet pitches yeast at 72° F (22° C) and allows the temperature to rise to about 77 to 79° F (25 to 26° C) during primary fermentation. Beer rests for three weeks at ambient temperature before Limet chills it to 36 to 37° F (2 to 3° C) for a week. He fills large bottles at the brewery and packages 330ml bottles at another brewery, both dosed with a second yeast. They condition at 77° F (25° C) for two weeks.

Including private-label beers, Limet brewed twenty-one recipes in 2004. That gave him an opportunity to use seven malts and numerous hops. All the malts come from Dingemans, but like other brewers he still mourns the decision by Interbrew to close the DeWolf-Cosyns maltings. "Ordinarily, malt is malt, but it's still difficult to lose that one," he said. Almost all the hops come from around Poperinge in West Flanders ("I have a guy who grows hops with love"), but he also likes to experiment and has dabbled with American Cascade.

By Belgian standards, Limet qualifies as a hophead. "There used to be fifty beers that made you go, like, 'Whoa!' and now you can count them on two hands," he said. "Everybody brews beer to sell. We have to sell beer, but my problem I have with some other brewers is they are brewing nine to ten beers, and everything is the same. The good things all get thrown overboard, and the bad stays. That is what has happened with hops. I miss that little bitterness that makes it a beer."

Limet seldom uses traditional bittering hops for bittering, preferring aroma hops with alpha acid levels below 6%. "I always make a blend for bittering," he said. For *Bink Tripel*, his newest offering in bottles, he mixed Challenger and East Kent Goldings pellets for bittering, adding Saaz (pellets again) for flavor.

Limet first brewed a tripel in 2003, selling it mostly on draft. "There are a lot of people who drink only tripel. There was a lot of demand, many people telling me I must make a tripel," he said. He aimed for something between *Westmalle Tripel* and *Chimay White*. Although not quite as attenuated as those two, *Bink Tripel* finishes properly dry and packs 38 IBUs of hop punch. Limet's recipe uses two kinds of Pilsener malt, along with sugar. "Common sugar, crystal sugar," he said. "If you make a strong beer with all malt, you can make a good beer, but you have a beer that is not so easy to digest."

He began regular production of the beer in 2005, calling the beer *Bink Tripel* for the American market and *Adelardus Tripel* at home. The Belgian version commemorates the opening of an abbey tower in nearby Saint Truiden. Saint Trudo founded the abbey in the seventh century, but according to local lore, every time that Saint Trudo tried to build a church it was pulled down by an interfering woman, until after passionate prayer by Saint

Bink Tripel

Original Gravity: 1.083 (20 °P)

Alcohol by Volume: 9%

Apparent Degree of Attenuation: 83%

IBU: 38

Malts: Pilsener (two varieties)

Adjuncts: Sucrose

Hops: East Kent Goldings and Challenger for bittering, Saaz for flavor

Yeast: Kerkom

Primary Fermentation: Yeast is pitched at 72° F (22° C), temperature allowed to reach 82 to 84° F (28 to 29° C), 10 days

Secondary Fermentation: 3 weeks at ambient temperature, 1 week at 36 to 37° F (2 to 3° C)

Also Noteworthy: Refermentation in the bottle

Trudo she was stricken with paralysis. Supporters helped raise money to restore the tower by commissioning Limet to brew a dubbel-style beer called *Adelardus Trudoabdijbier*. That label features a stylish illustration of a winking monk holding a beer, alongside a photograph of the tower.

Sampling the beer in another café on the way to *Het Vijgeblad*, Limet had to wait for his tripel to warm, letting the chill haze fade. ("That's good," an enthusiast told me later. "Those proteins are good for your health.") "This is a problem for all the pubs. All the (cooling) equipment is for pils beers," Limet said. "Westmalle does provide a cooler for its beers that is 50° F (10° C), but small brewers cannot afford such things."

Brewing a tripel seemed a natural for the Kerkom yeast. "It is much the same as Westmalle, we have practically the same yeast," Limet said. "I smell it at fermentation, ripe banana, and it needs time to calm down." One of Limet's first tasks at Kerkom was to clean up brewing practices in general, as well as yeast that had gone astray. "I put it under the microscope to get it clean. Now I keep it at two different breweries," he said. "People would visit and say, 'It is beautiful here so I came back, but the beer has been bad.' We are still overcoming that."

BRASSERIE CARACOLE

To see what it might have looked like when it took three men seven hours of continuous work to conduct a mash at Rochefort in 1900, visit Caracole in the village of Falmignoul, less than an hour's drive from Rochefort. Two men spend half a day milling

Saxo

Original Gravity: 1.065 (16 °P)

Alcohol by Volume: 8%

Apparent Degree of Attenuation: 85%

IBU: 21

Malts: Pilsener, unmalted wheat

Adjuncts: Sugar, 15% of fermentables

Spices: Coriander

Hops: Saaz

Yeast: Caracole

Primary Fermentation: Pitched at 77° F (25° C), rises or drops based on season, 7 to 10 days

Secondary Fermentation: 2 weeks at 41° F (5° C)

Also Noteworthy: Refermentation in bottle with primary yeast

malt for the next day's mash. They hoist a 25-kilogram bag above their heads to empty it into a mill made in 1913, then fill the bag with milled grain. One worker carries it across the room and lifts it up to the other on a platform, and he in turn totes it a short way before hoisting it again and depositing the grain into the mash tun.

No conveyor belt transports cases from the bottling line to the warm room, no forklifts haul things around. The old-fashioned circular lauter tun looks as if it were meant to be mechanically driven but isn't hooked up to a power source. How does it run? Guillaume Denayer, one of two regular brewery employees, considered the question. He lifted his left arm, made a muscle, and pointed to his bicep.

"We sleep very well," he said.

The kettles are wood fired, the last in Europe. "I think that is good for the flavor," said co-founder François Tonglet. Uneven firing creates hot spots in the bricked-in kettle, caramelizing the malt in longer boils. This particularly suits *Nostradamus*, a brooding 9.5% abv ale made with six malts.

Located in a stone building that is nearly two hundred years old, the brewery has a spiral staircase that runs from the cellar into a small attic, where Tonglet and Jean-Pierre Debras still have the equipment used in 1990, when they started Caracole in a 30-square-meter space in Namur. "We made seventy batches in four years; it was an opportunity to make trials for the beers we brew here," Tonglet said. Moving into the former Brasserie Moussoux, a producer of table beer that once had its own maltings, was a giant step up despite the modest surroundings. "It has always been used material for us. We are not rich enough to brew with new," Tonglet said. "It was a hobby. When we bought this building, we knew it would not stay a hobby."

Production grows every year, reaching 2,000 hectoliters (1,700 barrels) in 2004, with about half the beer sold outside of Belgium. A sign of the times, the shelves behind Tonglet's desk spill over with notebooks about details for shipping beer not only to the United States but to Japan and a variety of other countries. Michael Castelain, a local artist, designed the delightful labels, each featuring a snail. The brewery draws its name from the Spanish word for snail, because the people from the Namur region "do everything in our own way, and our accent is rather slow" Tonglet said. *Saxo*, a strong blonde, honors Adolphe Sax, who was born in nearby Dinant and developed the saxophone in the 1840s.

Caracole buys malts from Malterie du Château, supplementing those with organic malt from Dingemans. Hop pellets from Slovenia and the Czech Republic replaced flowers for the sake of consistency. The brewery has two yeast strains, one for most of the beers and another, more alcohol-tolerant strain for *Nostradamus*, repitching six to eight times and using the primary yeast for bottle-conditioning. Sugar, plain sucrose delivered in large bags, makes up about 15% of the fermentables in all the beers except *Troublette*, a wheat beer.

Caracole brews with the same water used by the town, drawn from two wells about 80 meters deep. "It is very rich in calcium, rather hard, very good water," Tonglet said. "We boil it the day before brewing to reduce the hardness." With the brewing calendar in sync, Caracole brews twice a week, thus making best use of water and wood. They'll bottle the next. Boiling water sets the mash at 145° F (63° C), and the wood fire raises it to

Nostradamus

Original Gravity: 1.083 (20 °P)

Alcohol by Volume: 9.5%

Apparent Degree of Attenuation: 75 to 80% (varies)

IBU: 20

Malts: Pilsener, Munich, 2 caramel, aromatic, wheat

Adjuncts: Sucrose (about 15% of fermentables)

Hops: Hallertau, Saaz

Yeast: More powerful of 2 Caracole yeasts

Primary Fermentation: Pitched at 77° F (25° C), rises or drops based on season, 7 to 10 days

Secondary Fermentation: 2 to 3 weeks at 41° F (5° C)

Also Noteworthy: Unlike many Caracole beers, this one has no spices; refermentation in the bottle with primary yeast

162° F (72° C). "We changed the use of the kettles. Before, they were doing everything by adding water. Now, we have one for water and one for boiling," Tonglet said.

Brew length depends on the beer, with *Troublette* yielding 48 hectoliters (41 barrels) and *Nostradamus* 32. Fermentation begins at 77° F (25° C), and the temperature goes up or down depending on the season. In the summer it may reach 86° F (30° C), and in the winter it will fall to 68° F (20° C). *Troublette* ferments in a week, while *Nostradamus* will take three.

"It is better to let the fermentation go like it will. We are very simple," Tonglet said.

Caracole lagers beer for two weeks at 41° F (5° C) before bottling. Bottles spend at least two weeks in the warm cellar below the brewhouse at 77° F (25° C).

EVERY BREWERY TELLS A STORY

The way the next five breweries present themselves, always leaning on tradition and often on innovation, emphasizes the diversity we expect from "strong Belgian ales."

Brouwerij De Koninck: The last independent brewery in Antwerp produces a beer as ubiquitous in that city as Budweiser is in St. Louis. Simply order a "bolleke" at about any place (hotel, café, etc.) that serves beer, and you'll be presented with a glass of classic De Koninck, a pale ale that for many defines the style. Alas, pale ales have not yet been explored in this series of books on Belgian brewing, and won't be here.

Because De Koninck recently began producing *De Koninck Blond*, you get a glimpse at how pale ale and blonde differ (for instance, notice the color or the use of sugar), the lesson stronger still if you have an opportunity to taste the two side by side.

De Koninck Pale

Original Gravity: 10.48 (12 °P)

Alcohol by Volume: 5%

Apparent Degree of Attenuation: 83%

IBU: 24

Malts: Pale, Vienna

Adjuncts: None

Hops: Saaz

Yeast: De Koninck yeast

Primary Fermentation: Pitched at 65° F (18° C), rises to 77° F (25° C), 4 to 5 days

Secondary Fermentation: 30° F (-1° C) for 2 to 3 weeks

Also Noteworthy: Bottle-conditioned, but no refermentation in the bottle

De Koninck makes its yeast available in a most unusual way at the Pilgrim café near the brewery, sending it over in buckets and serving it in shot glasses. Some drinkers take it straight, while others add it to their beer.

Established in 1833, De Koninck benefited from the same sort of link to Jean De Clerck as nearby Duvel and many Trappist breweries. De Clerck helped supervise modernization after World War II, when Antwerp still had nineteen breweries and De Koninck was but the fifth largest. In order to finance the project, Modeste Van den Bogaert sold off houses the brewery owned and used to rent to its workers. The current brewhouse, remodeled in 1995, produces 90,000 hectoliters (76,700 barrels) a year, making the brewery bigger than all but two Trappist operations.

De Koninck Blond

Original Gravity: 1.057 (14 °P)

Alcohol by Volume: 6%

Apparent Degree of Attenuation: 80%

IBU: 28

Malts: Pilsener

Adjuncts: Sucrose

Hops: Saaz

Yeast: De Koninck yeast

Primary Fermentation: Pitched at 65° F (18° C), rises to 77° F (25° C), 7 to 8 days

Secondary Fermentation: 30° F (-1° C) for 2 to 3 weeks

Also Noteworthy: Bottle-conditioned, but no refermentation in the bottle

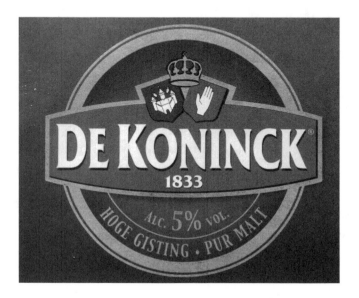

Brasserie des Rocs: Jean-Pierre Eloir, a tax inspector, and his brewing wife, Nathalie, founded the garage brewery in 1979, using material from the ruins of a nearby abbey. Although the brewery has no abbey connection, Nathalie brews distinctly abbeylike styles, and for twenty-five years the brewery called itself Abbaye des Rocs. It changed its name to avoid confusion about any monkish connection.

The brewery produces 4,000 hectoliters (3,400 barrels) per year with a 50-hectoliter brewhouse, boasting that recipes don't include sugar or similar adjuncts. Beers such as the popular *Grand Cru* include up to a half-dozen different malts, and are likely to be spiced with common additions (like coriander and ginger) and unusual ones (dandelion). The brewery doesn't filter and bottle-conditions with a second yeast.

Brouwerij Bosteels: Running one of two breweries in the smallish town of Buggenhout (Landtsheer, which brews the distinctive Malheur line, being the other), the Bosteels family operates with particular flare. Beer cafés sell *Kwak*, the first less-than-mainstream Belgian ale to be offered on tap in the United States (1995), in a distinctive "stirrup cup" that looks like a small yard of ale.

The brewery makes an abbey connection with *Tripel Karmeliet*. The recipe starts with barley, wheat, and oats; all unmalted as well as malted, and includes a solid dose of unspecified spices. The brewery named the beer *Karmeliet* because, it said, it found that the nearby Carmelite abbey made a three-grain beer in the 1600s. Antoine Bosteels, whose family has run the brewery for six generations, designed the elegant *Karmeliet* glass decorated with a frosted *fleur-de-lys*.

Tripel Karmeliet

Original Gravity: 1.081 (19.5 °P)

Alcohol by Volume: 8%

Apparent Degree of Attenuation: 84%

IBU: 20

Malts: Pilsener, wheat, oats, unmalted barley, unmalted wheat, unmalted oats

Adjuncts: Sucrose

Spices: Not specified, but coriander and others

Hops: Styrian Goldings, Saaz

Yeast: 2 yeasts

Primary Fermentation: 1 week at 75° F (24° C)

Secondary Fermentation: 4 weeks at 32° F (0° C)

Also Noteworthy: Refermentation in the bottle. The brewery describes its water as hard and makes only adjustments for pH

The brewery's third beer, calls *DeuS*, is riddled and disgorged in the Champagne style.

Brouwerij Het Anker: The Anker brewer, the Hotel Carolus, the brewery's Old World café, and a museum all operate within the complex beside a canal in Mechelen. Antique brewing equipment, some of it still in use, fills the brewery, the yard area, and the café. Even the breakfast room for the hotel—remodeled rooms that used to be part of the brewery—features old brewery signs, including one for a fake Trappist beer, called *Cardinal*, that Anker previously brewed. The brewery lays claim to being the oldest still operating in Belgium, with documents dating to 1369 and a history that predates that.

The Van Breedam family has owned the brewery since 1873 and converted it into one of the first modern steam-breweries. More recently, the beer quality improved after Charles Leclef took charge in 1990. He discontinued the use of a large coolship on top of the brewery, which looked magnificent but produced less-than-consistent beer. The giant open tank remains on display, attracting tourists who visit the museum, and on a clear day affords an excellent view of Mechelen.

Emperor of the Grand Cru

Original Gravity: 1.101 (23 °P)

Alcohol by Volume: 11%

Apparent Degree of Attenuation: 82%, will vary by up to 5% in any year

IBU: 24

Malts: Pilsener, caramel

Adjuncts: Maize

Spices: Secret

Hops: Challenger

Yeast: Het Anker

Primary Fermentation: Yeast is pitched at 68° F (20° C), rises to 77° F (25° C), 6 days

Secondary Fermentation: 2 weeks at 32° F (0° C)

Also Noteworthy: Brewed once a year, February 24, the birthday of Charles the Fifth; first brewed in 1999 at 8.5% abv, and known as *Cuvée van de Keizer* in Belgium. Refermentation in the bottle, with bottling at the Heineken-owned Affligem brewery

Het Anker brews several brands, the best known being the Gouden Carolus line, named after a coin with the head of the Holy Roman Emperor, Charles the Fifth (1500-1558). He spent much of his childhood in Mechelen when it was the capital of the Netherlands.

Brouwerij Sint-Bernardus: Saint Bernardus claims monastery links on both sides of the nearby French border. The brewery just outside of Watou operates in a building that first housed a cheese factory, established in the 1930s after the monks of the nearby French monastery Mont de Cats returned to their home. The Trappist monks started the business in Belgium during an unstable period in France.

St. Bernardus 12

Original Gravity: 1.090 (21.5 °P)

Alcohol by Volume: 10%

Apparent Degree of Attenuation: 83%

IBU: 22

Malts: Pilsener, black/dark malt "for aging stability"

Adjuncts: Beet sugar, dark caramel syrup (together nearly 20% of fermentables)

Hops: Target, Saaz

Yeast: Saint Bernardus yeast, could be original Westvleteren

Primary Fermentation: Yeast is pitched at 68° F (20° C), rises to 82 to 84° F (24° C), 5 to 7 days

Secondary Fermentation: 6 to 8 weeks at 50° F (10° C)

Also Noteworthy: Refermentation in the bottle, 330ml bottles bottled at brewery, 750ml bottles elsewhere; some versions pasteurized

After the monks at Westvleteren decided to rein in brewing in 1946, Saint Bernardus added a secondhand brewhouse to the property, and for forty-six years brewed the Saint Sixtus line of "Trappist" beers under contract. After Westvleteren ended the deal, Saint Bernardus continued with its own brands, extending the range and boosting production to 10,000 hectoliters (8,500 barrels) a year. Today it brews beers with no monastic influence—including *Grottenbier* under contract for Pierre Celis and a *wit* he helped formulate—but still uses recipes the brewery claims haven't changed since 1946.

Because the head brewer from Westvleteren helped set up the Saint Bernardus brewery, it seems likely he brought along the original Westvleteren yeast with the recipes. We can only guess how Saint Bernardus yeast today might have changed in sixty years. The brewery employs a second yeast in bottle-conditioning, with 330ml bot-tles conditioned at Saint Bernardus and 750ml bottles shipped elsewhere. Beers may be pasteurized, based on their destination.

After the contract between Saint Bernardus and Westvleteren ended, many cafés continued to describe the beers from Saint Bernardus as Trappist, leading to legal confrontations. As a result, Saint Bernardus bottles that formerly pictured a smiling monk hoisting a glass of beer now show the same fellow wearing a robe described as medieval rather than a monk's cowl.

A second Watou brewery, Van Eecke, also claims a connection to Mont des Cats. Its abbey-style *Het Kapittel* beers are named for "The Chapter" established by Mont des Cats monks during their exile from France.

Brewing in America

six

The American Way

A few months before Jeff Lebesch and Kim Jordan began selling New Belgium Brewing Company beers in 1991, they took samples of *Abbey* and *Fat Tire Amber Ale* to a bluegrass music festival in northern Colorado. "We were giving it away," Lebesch said, "it" being the *Abbey*. "And the response was decidedly underwhelming."

Until that day he thought *Abbey* would be the brewery's lead beer. He had been brewing test batches for about two years. "I was really proud of it," he said. "It was very enlightening to think the *Abbey* was not going to be our flagship."

In 2004, thirteen years after New Belgium opened in Fort Collins, Colorado, the brewery sold 331,500 barrels of beer (389,000 hectoliters), 35% more than all the Trappist breweries put together. "I'm usually one to plan those things out," said Lebesch, who used to be an engineer. "People ask me, 'What were you thinking?' I cannot remember having plans beyond the basement (where the first New Belgium brewing system was located)."

Fat Tire fueled the amazing run, but *Abbey* also has given Lebesch reason to be proud. The first time it captured gold at the Great American Beer Festival in 1993, the contest offered no separate category for Belgian-style beers; *Abbey* won best in Mixed Specialty, ahead of *Coors WinterFest* and *Spanish Peaks Raspberry Honey Ale*. The GABF created a Belgian category in 1994, and by 2004 *Abbey* had won eight more GABF medals, four of them gold.

The beer today differs considerably from the first test batch Lebesch brewed in 1989. He took aim at *Chimay Red*. "It was about 5% alcohol, 1.048 (12 °P). Apparently, I didn't know (*Chimay*) was a fair bit higher in starting gravity," Lebesch said, sounding properly amused. *Chimay Red*, 7.1% abv, starts at 1.061 (14.9 °P).

Michael Jackson wrote about being driven around Colorado by Lebesch back in 1990: "The road climbs into the Rockies, and, at 11,990 feet, crosses the Continental Divide. My recollection was that we pulled over at this point and cracked a bottle of *Chimay*. While we had our celebratory drink, Jeff told me he was a nursing an idea. He wanted to establish in the United States a microbrewery specializing in Belgian-style ales. At the time, no one had done this. Nor had anyone even thought of it, as far as I can recall. I told him that it was a great idea, but that America was not yet ready for such a venture."[1]

After Jackson told a similar story at a gathering at New Belgium, Lebesch pointed out they had not celebrated with *Chimay* but one of his test batches for *Abbey*. When Jackson went home and checked his notes he "found the beer hoppier than *Chimay*." Lebesch chuckled when the record showed he bittered that batch with American Willamette, Chinook, and Cascade hops.

[1] Jackson, "The Rockies' Rival to Rodenbach," *The Beer Hunter*, http://www.beerhunter.com/documents/19133-001604.html

Even though he laughs at himself today, Lebesch obviously knew more than most about Trappist-inspired beers. He recalls sitting in *Brugs Beertje,* a famous beer bar in Bruges. "Jan (De Bruyne, one of the owners) brought out a book on Belgian beer, and we were trying to read the description of *Chimay,*" Lebesch said. "I definitely remember reading 'Hallertauer.' That's the first time I finished the beer with Hallertauer."

Many others have since joined Lebesch in brewing Belgian-inspired beers. In this chapter, we'll visit microbreweries that focus on Belgian-type beers and also those that produce them as part of a broader portfolio. The brewers talk about ingredients and process as well as the specific beers they brew. In the chapters that follow, we'll look more closely at those ingredients, about the challenges of fermentation and the importance of proper packaging—everything it takes to successfully brew these beers on American soil.

Like Lebesch, many American brewers visit Belgium for inspiration. It's easy to imagine the more adventurous climbing into a car with Marc Limet of Brouwerij Kerkom and spending a Sunday afternoon banging about the countryside of Limberg, stopping along the way to sample beers, some from Kerkom and some not.

They would agree about brewing practices, and disagree. They would discuss mashing regimens and trade opinions about hop varieties. Perhaps the Americans would get to taste a beer Limet brewed for Kaffee Den Afgrond called *Boecht van den Afgrond.* "It means 'rubbish from the abyss,' " Limet would explain, the name designed to taunt drinkers who don't care for hops. He calculates the beer's IBUs at 50, about as high as anything brewed in Belgium.

"It's meant to fight the sweet beers," he'd tell them.

Ron Jeffries, who founded Jolly Pumpkin Artisan Ales in Dexter, Michigan, would be comfortable in the back seat. One of Jeffries' beers won gold at the 2004 GABF, although many of those he makes don't fit comfortably into style categories. He and Limet surely would debate using spices. Jeffries does with a certain zeal, Limet doesn't and has strong opinions about many of the spiced beers brewed in Belgium.

Jeffries can be equally hard on his own countrymen. "A lot of what has been made in the States is not at all what these beers taste like in Belgium," he said. "What I'm trying to do here is going against that sweeter beer trend."

Listen carefully. There's an echo.

SINGLE- (AND DUBBEL-) MINDED

New Belgium Brewing wasn't the only American microbrewery to open in the early 1990s that is devoted to brewing Belgian-inspired beer. Unibroue began selling its beer in Canada in 1990, and in 1991 Belgian brewing legend Pierre Celis launched the Celis Brewery in Austin, Texas. Others have followed, always offering a cross-section of styles brewed in Belgium. Here's a closer look at two of them.

Brewery Ommegang

An American importing company and Belgian brewers created Brewery Ommegang in a partnership that merged cultures. The brewery itself sits in the countryside outside Cooperstown, New York, home of the Baseball Hall of Fame. Although it opened in 1997, you don't have to squint too hard to see a Belgian farmhouse circa 1880. A *bona fide* tourist attraction, the brewery provides many Americans with their first look at open fermentation or a warm room for bottle-conditioning.

Ommegang

Original Gravity: 10.76 (18.5 °P)

Alcohol by Volume: 8.5%

Apparent Degree of Attenuation: 81%

IBU: 20

Malts: Pilsener, amber, aromatic

Adjuncts: Glucose

Spices: 5 (various)

Hops: Styrian Goldings, Czech Saaz

Yeast: House yeast, acquired from Belgium

Primary Fermentation: 4 to 5 days, rising to 77° F (25° C)

Secondary Fermentation: 2 weeks at 31° F (-1° C)

Also Noteworthy: Refermentation in the bottle with primary yeast

"The open fermenter is eye candy for the tourists," said brewmaster Randy Thiel. "It's like, 'Wow, this is a living process.' "As the brewery has expanded, cylindro-conicals have been added. Thiel hasn't found they change the character of Ommegang's beer, but he wouldn't want to give up his open fermenter. "It's such a great utility for harvesting yeast. I would love to be able to do what they do at Moortgat (top cropping from closed fermenters)," he said.

Duvel Moortgat bought out American importing partner Vanberg & DeWulf in 2003. V&D started importing *Duvel* into the United States in 1982, and owners Don Feinberg and Wendy Littlefield were among the first and most eloquent promoters of Belgian beer in the United States. Trained as a microbiologist, Thiel was an avid homebrewer and a graduate of the University of California at Davis master brewers' course when he started at Ommegang. Working with Belgian brewer Bert de Wit, he learned to brew the "Belgian way" from the beginning.

"I didn't have to unlearn brewing things," he said. "What I did have to unlearn is the way I looked at beer and tasted beer. Don Feinberg taught me a lot about approaching flavor. How to taste with my taste buds and with my heart." Feinberg conducted tours with equal enthusiasm. He explained the process with care, from blending batches to the challenges of bottle-conditioning, while keeping the focus on the beer. "My feeling about artisanal is that if your approach is more product-oriented than process-oriented, you are on the way to artisanal," he said. Trays of spices on display out beside the boiling kettles made perfect props for Feinberg. He would pick up a handful of coriander and close his eyes as he brought it to his nose. "When it comes with a seed cover, we want that in the beer. It acts like tannins in wine," he said.

Ommegang sales grew more than 20% in 2004, to 5,300 barrels (6,200 hectoliters), and early in 2005 Thiel oversaw more construction and expansion to boost the capacity of the warm room by two-thirds and add fermenters. With a new outdoor cylindro-conical tank in place, a little more than 10% of fermentation takes place in the open. "If anything, our open fermenter gives us more problems," Thiel said. "It is kind of shallow and doesn't have natural convections."

Ommegang draws water, relatively low in both calcium and bicarbonate, from a 290-foot-deep well. It chlorinates the water, not only because of health department rules but because that helps precipitate soluble iron in the water. Then it dechlorinates brewing water through an active carbon filter.

Brewery Ommegang resides on what was once a 136-acre hop farm.

Recipes blend domestic malts and a range from Dingemans in Belgium. All beers start with a Pilsener base malt, with a range of amber, caramel, aromatic, and dark roasted malts used in the abbey-influenced beers. Hops include Styrian Goldings and Czech Saaz. Thiel draws from a bank of eight spices. "You don't make a 'spiced beer' if you are brewing a Belgian beer," he said, setting the rules. "We are trying to create a gastronomic experience. Spices should play the background role for the beer, to be a supporting character. When you put in too many spices, you ruin the drinkability of the beer."

As at most Belgian breweries, Ommegang conducts a step-infusion mash. Mashing lasts two hours, lautering two hours, and boiling two hours. The brewery adds sugar during the boil. "We started using clear candi sugar (rock crystals) back in 1997," Thiel said. "We quickly realized that it wasn't a good idea. Clear candi sugar is just crystallized sucrose; more water content and more expensive. We temporarily switched to beet sugar (granular sucrose) and eventually switched to corn sugar (glucose, a.k.a. dextrose) without any change in flavors."

Fermentation begins at 64° F (18° C) and rises as high as 77° F (25° C) during the course of four or five days, whether in the open fermenter or in closed. The brewery pitches at a "traditional

American micro" rate of 1 million cells per milliliter per degree Plato. For instance, *Ommegang* is pitched at 18.5 million cells per milliliter. That's considerably higher than at Moortgat (7.5 million per milliliter for *Duvel*), and Thiel and Moortgat brewmaster Hedwig Neven have discussed making changes at Ommegang. "When we've tried to pitch lower, we don't get complete attenuation," Thiel said.

Thiel achieves slightly better attenuation in the conicals, but that's not what other brewers want to talk about. "They usually can't believe we aren't destroying the beer at that (fermentation) temperature," he said. "Honestly, if we ferment it lower it will be underattenuated, sugary, sweet, and it's a potential microbiological nightmare. There have been times when we had a breakdown in the cooling system on the weekend, and when I came in on Monday the beer was at 33° C (91° F). Lo and behold, it tasted fine. Those types of experiences have made me not afraid of higher temperatures."

Ommegang chose the yeast strain from a yeast bank in Belgium. "We picked it for the ester profile and phenolics, and because it could ferment high-gravity beers. We like it because it doesn't come across as being the same yeast in all our beers," Thiel said. The brewery first planned to let its yeast develop house flavors, letting it go as many generations as possible without renewing it. That did not turn out to be a good idea. "Being a microbiologist, after sixty generations I didn't feel comfortable with that," Thiel said. "We had a beer with no esters and bad bottle-conditioning. At that point we decided to limit it to seven generations." He put the yeast under a microscope and made colony selections that leave him with a yeast that flocculates properly and has the flavor profile that first attracted Ommegang.

After primary, beers rests two weeks at 31° F (-1° C). Workers filter the beer before adding sugar and fresh yeast. "We bottle at 0° C and have twenty-four hours to get it to 25° C, or we run the risk of selling flat beer with sugar in it," Thiel said. Lower-alcohol beers are dosed with about 1 million cells per milliliter, while bigger ones such as *Ommegang* and *Three Philosophers* get 2 to 3 million cells per milliliter. The brewery targets 7.5 grams of CO_2 per liter (3.75 volumes) in the bottle.

Thiel values using fresh, viable yeast (from top cropping) as much in bottle-conditioning as for primary fermentation. "You are putting the yeast in a very harsh environment of alcohol and CO_2 with only a little glucose sugar, and asking it to gobble (the glucose) up like it has a full meal," he said. "It's not afforded a lag phase, it's not in a wort with dissolved oxygen. We put it in the bottle, and it has to start assimilating. Here is a simple sugar, and we tell it, 'You don't have any oxygen, and we expect you to do the job.' "

Bottles spend between one week and two in the floor-heated warm room. The brewery added an additional ceiling heater during expansion, pumping heat to the floor. "The radiant heat was good at maintaining temperature, but not if you wanted to raise it," Thiel said.

In 2004 Thiel became the first American brewer knighted by the Belgian brewers' organization *Chevalerie de Fourquet* ("Knights of the Mashing Fork"), receiving the award during a celebration held annually in Brussels. An hour-long parade blocks traffic around the busy Grand'Place, with members of the Knights of the Mashing Fork marching in colorful robes to the ceremony, which itself goes on for some time. "It almost brings a tear to my eye seeing how the Belgian community takes so much pride in this organization," Thiel said.

Allagash Brewing

Nobody offered Rob Tod a manual when he started to brew Belgian-inspired beers. He was left to figure out much of it on his own. "There are things that happen (in the brewery) where I can call two hundred guys for advice. With these beers there's no one to call," Tod said. Almost from the beginning, Tod experimented with packaging beers in 750ml bottles. "We'd change yeast, use different bottles," he said. "We'd try one thing at a time, crowns versus corks, different amounts of yeast, a different kind of sugar."

More than ten years after starting Allagash Brewing Company in Portland, Maine, as a one-man operation, Tod hasn't quit exploring. "One of the things about brewing Belgian beers is the whole style encourages experimentation," he said. "I'm excited about developing a library of beers."

Tod worked at Otter Creek Brewing Company in Vermont in 1994, when he sampled *Celis White* for the first time. "People were traveling, and they'd bring back beer. Every few weeks we'd have a tasting," Tod said. On June 30, 1994, he left Otter Creek to start Allagash Brewing. One year to the day later, he put *Allagash White* on tap at Portland's venerable Great Lost Bear. It has been the bar's top-selling beer ever since.

"I didn't know if we'd do one beer or ten beers," Tod said, "but I knew we'd focus on Belgian beer." His second beer was a dubbel, at first sold only on draft. He calls it *Allagash Double Ale* in 12-ounce bottles, and *Allagash Dubbel Reserve* in 750ml bottles. Until 2004 the *Reserve* refermented in bottles, while the brewery

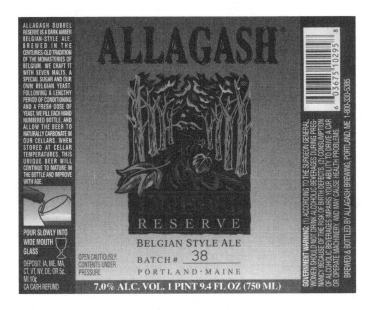

force-carbonated the *Double*. Now both undergo refermentation, although the *Reserve* has 3.8 volumes of CO_2 in the bottle and the *Double* 2.4, because the 12-ounce bottles are not rated to hold higher volumes safely.

"We want to make each beer unique within the lineup of beers we do," Tod said. "We try not to match other beers in the market. We didn't try to go after any one beer. I'm not out to duplicate anything; we try to do another thing. On the *Dubbel* I was shooting for the drier side, with some chocolate. I wanted customers to be able to drink two or three and not feel overwhelmed." The *Dubbel*, like a tripel that followed, passes the Belgian "digestible" test and is an excellent beer to serve with food. Allagash teams with the Institute for Culinary Education in New York City for a "Cookin' With Allagash" contest. This event features some of the United States' up-and-coming chefs concocting original recipes, all made with Allagash beers.

When he created the *Dubbel* in 1996, Tod couldn't find a good source for dark candi sugar (rocks). Instead he used lighter-colored rock candy from a regional supplier and added more dark malts to the recipe—the Pilsener base supplemented with 20 °L and 120 °L crystal and roasted malt. "We've always tried to use as many domestic ingredients as possible," he said. While at Otter Creek, he developed a relationship with Briess Malt & Ingredients that continues today. Allagash uses American-grown hops of noble heritage as well as Czech Saaz. Tod takes soft water from Lake Sebago, which he dechlorinates before brewing.

"The key is a Belgian yeast; you have to have a Belgian yeast," Tod said. Looking at his proprietary yeast under a microscope, Tod sees more than one strain. He has grown to know it well and followed the yeast's lead in adjusting fermentation practices. "We pitch it cooler, and let it rise," he said. "Over the years we moved to using the rising temperature, because our yeast needs it to have a strong finish. But if we let it get too warm early, we tend to get a fruity, estery beer.

"It must be like wine yeast. I've had some wines where I've thought, 'I've tasted this in a beer. There are some of the same compounds.' "

He uses four yeasts in *Allagash Four*, brewed for the first time in 2004. "Everybody told us, 'You have to do a quad,' " Tod said, talking about the "quadrupel" style that's not quite a style. Allagash brews its version with four malts, four hops, four yeasts, and four sugars, and a fermentation regimen nearly as rigorous as Duvel's bottle-conditioning.

Allagash mashes date sugar with the malts, then adds light candi sugar (rocks), dark candi sugar (rocks), and light golden molasses in the kettle. The beer begins fermentation at 1.078 (18.9 °P), and the first yeast will complete about two-thirds of the work.

"At that point we bring the starting gravity up six points (with sugar) and add a second actively fermenting yeast, and let it go as far as it can," Tod said. "We'll condition that for a week, storing it at fermentation temperature. At this point the yeast is incapable of vigorous fermentation. We'll transfer it to a second tank, raise it another six points, and add a third active strain. We'll let that continue, then condition two to three weeks. We filter out the first three yeasts, add a fourth, and sugar and bottle it."

The beer finishes with about 10% alcohol—going from 1.090 (21.6 °P) to 1.015 (3.8 °P). Tod estimates the bitterness at 30 IBU. "We haven't even calculated it," he said. "At this stage we look at the levels of (alpha acids) we've added to other beers and have a feel for how much hops to put in."

The results delight him. "Each fermentation adds complexity and layers of flavor," he said.

Allagash grew to 4,050 barrels in 2004, with the last quarter its strongest in history before the first quarter of 2005 topped that. The brewery expanded within the industrial space it has occupied since 1995, in 2004 adding a dedicated warm room as well as a retail area with beers aging in barrels on display. *Curieux* became the first release in a barrel-aged series. Tod took his tripel and aged it for eight weeks in bourbon barrels. *Odyssey*, 10% abv with substantial wheat malt and some roasted malt, followed. The beer aged for a year, a portion of the time in stainless steel and a portion in new American oak barrels.

White remains Allagash's flagship beer, but Tod's well on the way to developing that library of beers. His goal sparks memories of Anneke Benoit standing in the Claustrum at Westvleteren's *In De Vrede*, pointing to an antique book on display and saying, "If the monks wanted to read a book (hundreds of years ago), they had to write it first." Tod creates equally original volumes.

EXPANDING HORIZONS

Whether they are called dubbels or doubles, tripels or triples, or perhaps something else that conjures up images of Belgium, more different Trappist-inspired beers are brewed in the United States than in Belgium, most of them served on draft in brewpubs. A Belgian brewing family started one of them, Saint Sebastiaan Belgian Microbrewery near St. Petersburg, Florida, and it focuses entirely on Belgian beers.

For the most part, though, circumstances limit pub brewers to one-offs or irregular regulars when it comes to offering Belgian-inspired beer, part of a portfolio that may include just about any style of beer. This book focuses on distributed beers simply because they are distributed, and there's a better chance for readers to sample the beers described. However, we shouldn't overlook brewpubs' influence. They introduce beer drinkers to styles they may never have tried. It seems far easier to try a sample-size of a beer that is dark, funky, and strong than investing in a bottle that might cost double digits. Also, even when limited to serving beers on draft that were originally meant to be bottled with high volumes of CO_2, many pub brewers make outstanding examples of the styles.

By the mid-1990s many packaging microbreweries began to experiment with beers of Belgian heritage. "We were looking for a logical extension in terms of expanding the horizons of our customers here in Fort Bragg and in California," said North Coast Brewing Company brewmaster Mark Ruedrich, recalling the decision to create *PranQster*. "We'd gotten over our fear of having another yeast strain around. When we finally brewed it, we were interested in doing it as a fun thing and as an academic exercise as brewers. It was another challenge."

Tripels on Main Street

One of the challenges of brewing abbey and other Belgian-inspired beers remains coaxing yeast into working the first time out of the box, then giving higher-alcohol beers time to develop. "Brewers using these yeasts on a regular basis have a decided advantage in being able to tailor yeast and malt profiles," said one Great American Beer Festival judge. Nonetheless, pub brewers, often limited to brewing a single batch and then moving on, still make award-winning beers.

Main Street Brewing Company of Corona, California, captured two medals at the 2004 GABF, one for *Bishop's Tipple Trippel* and another for *Katarina Wit*. You can probably guess the styles.

"My first few batches were too sweet. Now I mash at a lower temperature and pitch more yeast," said brewer Bob Kluver, talking about how his tripel has changed since he first brewed it. He boosted apparent attenuation from 72 to 78%.

He uses White Labs WLP500 (comparable to Wyeast 1214). "On my notes I wrote, this yeast has a big banana nose if you ferment it above 65° F (18° C), but that it dissipates with time," he said. (*Specifications on next page.*)

Bishop's Tippel Trippel

Original Gravity: 1.090 (21.7 °P)

Alcohol by Volume: 9%

Apparent Degree of Attenuation: 78%

IBU: 48

Malts: Pale, CaraPils

Adjuncts: Candi sugar (rocks, about 10% of fermentables)

Hops: Perle, Saaz

Yeast: White Labs WLP500

Primary Fermentation: Yeast is pitched at 70° F (21° C), then temperature is reduced to 62° F (17° C)

Secondary Fermentation: One week at 33° F (1° C)

Also Noteworthy: 10-barrel pitch for 7-barrel batch

Ruedrich took his inspiration from a picture in Michael Jackson's *New World Guide to Beer* (Running Press, 1988) that showed a poster advertising a *lambic*. "Sometimes it is as simple as that," he said. "I looked at that picture and thought, 'God, that's a pretty beer. It is just beautiful. I want our beer to look like that.' " As part of the exercise, North Coast rounded up all the Belgian yeast it could find. "From Wyeast, UC-Davis, the scrapings from dregs, everything we could," Ruedrich said. Eventually, he settled on two yeasts to use in tandem in *PranQster*. "The idea of working with a yeast, learning it, and learning what it will do is very important. You've got to be willing to take a long time to get to know its ins and outs."

PranQster

Original Gravity: 1.070 (16.9 °P)

Alcohol by Volume: 7.4%

Apparent Degree of Attenuation: 80%

IBU: 19

Malts: American two-row, wheat, unmalted wheat, Munich

Adjuncts: Invert sugar (about 10% of fermentables)

Hops: Tettnang, Liberty

Yeast: 2 yeasts

Primary Fermentation: Yeast pitched at 67° F (19° C), rises to 72° F (22° C), temperature lowered 10 degrees per day after 2 weeks

Secondary Fermentation: At least 2 weeks at 33° F (1° C), until cell count is low enough for bottling

Also Noteworthy: Bottle-conditioned, not re-yeasted

Ruedrich sounded a bit whimsical, but he isn't the only brewer to use human terms when describing what he was looking for in yeast: "Flavor and fermentation characteristics. Fruit, pepper, clove. Personality. Independent and interesting, but able to work well as part of a team." In the end, Ruedrich settled on two yeasts, with one pitched at 65% of volume.

PranQster has medaled in both the World Beer Cup and Great American Beer Festival as a tripel, and has been honored as a strong pale ale in other competitions. Ruedrich hasn't always been satisfied looking for a competition category to put the beer in, but decided not to let that bother him. "One of the things that's appealing about the Belgian styles is the freedom. You kind of get fired up from all that," he said. "It's expected to be idiosyncratic."

Adam Avery of Avery Brewing Company in Boulder, Colorado, wasn't sure what to expect when he brewed *The Reverend* in 2000, naming it as a tribute to the life of sales manager Tom Boogaard's grandfather, an ordained Episcopal minister. "I thought if I could sell four hundred cases that would be great," Avery said. Brewed with borrowed yeast, the first batch had attenuation problems, dropping from a starting gravity of 1.110 (25.9 °P) to a sweetish 1.030 (7.6 °P). "We weren't expecting anything. We just said, 'Let's make a big beer,'" Avery said. "We learned a lot from that one."

Now Avery ferments *Salvation*, a golden strong ale, with Wyeast 3787, and then harvests the yeast to use in *The Reverend*, which starts at 1.093 (22.2 °P) and finishes at 1.018 (4.6 °P). It

Salvation

Original Gravity: 1.080 (19.3 °P)

Alcohol by Volume: 9%

Apparent Degree of Attenuation: 85%

IBU: 28

Malts: American 2-row, 2 caramel (8 °L and 20 °L)

Adjuncts: Clear candi sugar (rocks)

Hops: Styrian Goldings

Yeast: Wyeast 3787

Primary Fermentation: Yeast pitched and held at 72° F (22° C) for 7 days

Secondary Fermentation: 2 weeks at ambient temperature

Also Noteworthy: Filtered and force-carbonated

became Avery's best-selling beer in 22-ounce bottles, surpassing popular *Hog Heaven Barley Wine*, and acted as the impetus for creating a series of high-alcohol beers even bigger than those in Avery's Holy Trinity (*Hog Heaven*, *The Reverend*, and *Salvation*). Avery calls *The Beast*, also brewed with yeast first used in *Salvation*, a *Grand Cru*, and it reaches 18.1% abv. In late 2004 Avery continued on the experimental track, putting each of the Trinity beers in different types of wine barrels. *The Reverend* aged in Opus One barrels, *Salvation* in Chardonnay casks.

"We found out we could make a beer that wasn't super hoppy, that would get people's attention, and that they'd drink," said Avery, who continues to offer a line of beers that spans from traditional English ales to American hop monsters.

The Reverend commands attention. All Avery beers start with American two-row from its silo, then *The Reverend* includes five Belgian malts from Dingemans, including Special "B." "We use real Belgian candi sugar (dark rocks)," Avery said. "We could probably make it cheaper, but it is easy to get, and it tastes so good. I'm paying $3.50 a pound or something stupid like that, and I could get the same gravity for 49 cents."

Avery calls the pitching rate for *The Reverend* TMTC ("Too many to count") in well-oxygenated wort that he'll hold at 72° F (22° C) throughout fer- 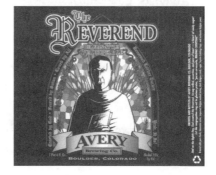 mentation. "If we try to go lower, the fermentation starts arresting, and we have problems finishing *The Reverend*," Avery said. "This gives us the flavor we want and gets it done in the time we want." The gravity drops to 1.025 (6.3 °P) in the first three days, but takes another four to five days to reach terminal gravity of 1.018 (4.6 °P). Everything takes place in a unitank, with secondary lasting two weeks at the ambient temperature in the brewery. Avery then crashes the beer below freezing and filters it to remove the yeast before letting it sit again at an ambient temperature. He polish-filters all beers before bottling. "I think bottle-conditioning is really hard," Avery said. "I like brilliant beer, particularly for the Holy Trinity."

In New Jersey, Flying Fish Brewing Company made a dubbel one of its core beers from the beginning, along with three English-style ales. "When we opened in 1996, there were

Flying Fish Dubbel

Original Gravity: 1.067 (16.4 °P)

Alcohol by Volume: 7%

Apparent Degree of Attenuation: 80%

IBU: 18

Malts: 2-row pale, Munich, CaraPils, Special "B," chocolate

Adjuncts: Candi sugar (rocks)

Hops: Styrian Goldings

Yeast: House Belgian yeast

Primary Fermentation: 3 days with peak temperature of 68° F (20° C)

Secondary Fermentation: 14 to 21 days, temperature dropping to 32° F (0° C)

Also Noteworthy: Refermentation in the bottle, kraeusened with primary yeast

very few American breweries doing Belgian styles," said founder Gene Muller. "We saw that as an opportunity no one else was really exploring. They were also a style we were very interested in. Now, practically every brewer brews Belgian styles, which I think is a great thing."

Flying Fish since has added two other Belgian-inspired beers to its seasonal offerings, while continuing to refine the *Dubbel*. "When we first started brewing our *Abbey Dubbel*, we originally fermented with our house (English ale) yeast, and then after primary fermentation introduced a Belgian style," Muller said. "Just because in our area we were not sure how folks would respond to the unique Belgian profiles. After about two years we started fermenting completely with our Belgian strain. We've subsequently increased the alcohol by adding more candi sugar to give it a little bit more complexity. We believe in helping our consumers' palates evolve by evolving our Belgian styles."

MONKS, *DAMNATION*, AND *TEMPTATION*

By the time Russian River Brewing Company opened in Santa Rosa, California, in the spring of 2004, brewer Vinnie Cilurzo already had a reputation for making outstanding Belgian-inspired beers, but he wasn't prepared for the response those beers would get in the brewpub. "To be honest, I'd hoped they'd be 15% (of sales)," he said. Instead, almost from the beginning, Cilurzo's interpretation of Belgian styles accounted for 35 to 40% of sales.

"We're using the pub as an educational platform," he said. "In flavor profile, people are trading up (in flavor and price) from the normal stuff that is typically seen in the brewpub."

Damnation

Original Gravity: 1.066 (16.1 °P)

Alcohol by Volume: 7%

Apparent Degree of Attenuation: 82%

IBU: 25

Malts: Continental Pilsener, American 2-row

Adjuncts: Dextrose

Hops: Styrian Goldings, Sterling

Yeast: Proprietary version of White Labs WLP500

Primary Fermentation: Upward rising, beginning at 64° F (18° C), 7 days

Secondary Fermentation: 32° F (0° C), 10 days

Also Noteworthy: Refermentation in the bottle with second yeast

Cilurzo brews nearly a dozen beers whose names end in "tion," each taking inspiration from Belgium, although some are not like any you'd find on the continent. He started with *Damnation*. Cilurzo knew that he wanted to brew Belgian-style beers when he was at Blind Pig Brewing Company in Southern California, but at that time his fermenters were large, food-grade plastic tanks. "We stuck to one yeast," Cilurzo said. A local homebrewer kept bringing in samples of Belgian-style beers. "About that time I had *PranQster* for the first time and went, 'Wow!' I started to take the homebrew recipes and play with them at home."

He thought *Damnation* would be dark, rather than golden. "I used dark sugar and was thinking that would darken it up. I was wrong, but it was so good that I decided to stick with it," he said. Next, he needed a name. Korbel Champagne Cellars owned Russian River at the time, and Cilurzo was driving from its location in Guerneville to his home in Healdsburg. "I can still remember where I was, making the turn onto Redwood Highway," he said, when a song titled "Hell" by the band Squirrel Nut Zippers came on the radio. In the song the Zippers spell out "damnation." "I instantly knew we could do a whole line of 'tion' beers," Cilurzo said. The song is still on the jukebox at the Russian River pub.

When Cilurzo and his wife, Natalie, visited Belgium in 1999, they stayed within the walls at Chimay. He was taken with *Dorée*, the monks' beer, and later *Westmalle Extra* and the *Westvleteren 4* (which was about to be discontinued). "We'd eat in silence, I'd drink my beer and steal a little of Natalie's," he said. "I was trying to break down the beer in my head." Soon he brewed *Redemption*, a 4.8% abv beer, for Russian River.

He started making adjustments as soon as he brewed his first commercial batch, a one-off dubbel called *California Abbey Ale*, in 1998 at Russian River. "For me, the biggest change has been the addition of more hops, more hops than traditionally would be added to a Belgian ale," he said. "This was done mainly to accommodate the palate of the beer-buying public. I thought (the *Abbey*) was fantastic, but it didn't sell. In fact, I think Toronado in San Francisco was the only bar that took it. That in and of itself was a sign of the times."

When Korbel decided to get out of the beer business in 2002, the Cilurzos bought the brand and moved the brewery to Santa Rosa. "As Belgian styles became more a part of our main lineup, we had to start thinking of the economics of the brew," he said. "The easiest place to do that while not hurting the flavor profile was with the sugars we use. Initially, I used Belgian candi sugar (rock crystals), which proved to be too expensive. Now we use turbinado sugar (although dextrose in darker beers)."

He looks at his grain bill with the same practical eye, mixing continental Pilsener with more affordable American two-row for his base, then adding specialty malts from Castle (Malterie du Château) in Belgium. "I hate to think in the economic terms, but there's the reality of it," he said. He'll continue to experiment with different base malts from both the United States and Belgium.

Regulars at the brewpub noticed changes in *Damnation* throughout the first year in Santa Rosa, as Cilurzo experimented with a different yeast in about every other batch. "I've gone back to my original," he said. "It's a private strain of White Labs 500. When homebrewers ask me about yeast, that's where I steer them. The one thing I see with other yeasts, is that I'm getting more phenolics than I want. I want our beer to be clean, bright, and dry as it ages out."

He also changed the fermentation regimen for *Damnation*. "We've really lowered the temperature, starting in the mid-60s then letting it ramp up on the fourth day by turning off the (fermenter) jackets," he said. "In the end it only gets to 68° F (20° C). I've found that's a good way to control the fruitiness. If you don't want too many phenolics, then your compromise is that you get big fruit. My beers may be fruity young, when they are in the tap. But we've got six years' experience with this yeast in the bottle."

He uses a single-infusion mash at 149 to 151° F (65 to 66° C), looking for good attenuation. "Coming from a wine background, I got an understanding that you can have a dry wine that is fruity," Cilurzo said. His parents started a winery when he was 8 years old, and he spent the better part of sixteen years as a cellar rat. "The big thing is knowing what the yeast can do," he said. "(Wyeast) 1056 is still our base yeast (for non-Belgian beers). You let that get over 68° F (20° C), 70 tops, you start spitting out diacetyl. You have to understand what the yeast can do and what it cannot do."

Vinnie Cilurzo draws a sample of Temptation. A final step before bottling is blending batches, something he learned in his family's winery. Photo courtesy of Natalie Cilurzo.

He operates comfortably in Wine Country and can talk at length about the business practices and strategies of wineries. He appreciates the irony that he turned to brewing when he was 24 because he discovered he could make beer in twenty-one days, and now some of his beers need much longer to finish. "I'm back to taking a year to make a fermented beverage," he said. *Temptation* spends nine months after primary fermentation in used Chardonnay barrels. "It started with the idea I wanted to make a blonde barrel-aged beer," Cilurzo said. *Temptation* ferments with Belgian yeast (White Labs WLP510, which is an offspring of Orval's primary yeast), then Cilurzo adds *Brettanomyces* in secondary, making the beer interesting to taste alongside of *Orval*. Although *Temptation* has won medals as a Belgian-style beer, nothing in Belgium tastes quite like it.

"I love lambics, so I decided to take one component of lambic and do that in this beer. The idea of extracting some of the wine flavor (from the barrels) happened on its own," Cilurzo said. A growing number of American brewers use wild yeasts in brewing, but most still worry about turning even the more mainstream Belgian yeast strains loose in their brewery. "To me, it's the opposite. You have to embrace it," Cilurzo said. "It's like a dog. When you are afraid of a dog, he senses that. You can't let (the yeast) sense you are afraid. Of course, we keep different hoses, different pumps and gaskets, rubber, two of everything. But to me, the thought of the *Brett* getting out of control adds to the excitement of it."

Russian River serves *Temptation* and other Belgian-style beers in a goblet. "We have a stemmed goblet that we use for just the Belgian-style ales," Cilurzo said. "We use a smaller version and a larger version, depending on the alcohol con-

Temptation

Original Gravity: 1.062 (15.2 °P)

Alcohol by Volume: 6.15% after primary, 7.25% after 9 months in barrels

Apparent Degree of Attenuation: 84%

IBU: 27

Malts: Continental Pilsener, unmalted wheat

Hops: Styrian Goldings, Sterling

Yeast: White Labs WLP510

Primary Fermentation: 72° F (22° C) for 5 days, then turn off the jackets

Ongoing Fermentation: 32° F (0° C) for 3 weeks, then it is fined and racked into used Chardonnay barrels, and 3 different strains of *Brettanomyces* are added. While the beer is aging for 9 months, it is topped every 3 weeks with *Sanctification* (another beer). Once the beer has completed its barrel-aging process, it is racked and blended with a small amount of old *Temptation* and *Depuration* (blonde ale aged in Chardonnay barrels with 60 pounds of grapes in each barrel).

Also Noteworthy: Refermentation in the bottle

---

tent. It's great to walk out into the brewpub and get an instant snapshot of what people are drinking, because I see the goblets on the table." The best-selling beer in the brewpub remains *Russian River India Pale Ale*, and the second-best-selling *Damnation*. Among distributed beers, *Pliny the Elder*, an imperial IPA, sells best.

In the pub *Damnation* sells for the same price as an average beer. Only higher-alcohol beers, or those that otherwise cost more to produce, are more expensive. "If we priced (Belgian styles) higher, the consumer may not be as open to purchasing the beer," Cilurzo said. "At the end of the day, there have to be some of these styles that are lower in alcohol, and that are accessible to the average, everyday beer drinker. One of the neatest things I see in our brewpub is some big, burly Harley-Davidson type drinking a Belgian-style ale out of a goblet. I can already see that in our region, people are getting what I'm trying to do. Of course, we have an advantage being in the California Wine Country."

AUBERGE DE POTEAUPRÉ

Lest there be any doubt about the inspiration behind the beer now known as *New Belgium Abbey*, consider that Jeff Lebesch's first three homebrewed batches were called *Auberge de Poteaupré*, which is the name of the inn Chimay operates about a quarter mile from the monastery.

The first version used about half extract syrup along with wheat malt, crystal 40, chocolate, pale, and Munich. It was bittered with Chinook, Perle, and Fuggles, and fermented with yeast Lebesch cultured from a Chimay bottle. It started at 1.048 (12 °P) and finished at 1.016 (4 °P). Lebesch's tasting notes were concise: "A lovely beer."

Today *Abbey* starts at 1.063 (15.5 °P) and finishes at (1.010) 2.6 °P, but is still fermented with the "house abbey" yeast. "What I learned later is that Chimay could get kind of wild," Lebesch said, "so who knows how reflective what I got out of that bottle was of Chimay? I was doing all my culturing from bottles then, keeping them on plates in the house. Somewhere in the early 1990s, I did a major cleanup of our yeast. It really changed the character of the beer."

New Belgium Abbey

Original Gravity: 1.063 (15.5 °P)

Alcohol by Volume: 7%

Apparent Degree of Attenuation: 83%

IBU: 24

Malts: Pale, Munich, caramel 80, chocolate, CaraPils

Hops: Target, Willamette, Liberty

Yeast: House abbey yeast

Primary Fermentation: Yeast pitched at 63° F (17° C), rises to 70° F (21° C), 7 days

Secondary Fermentation: 2 weeks at 30° F (-1° C)

Also Noteworthy: Refermentation in the bottle with second yeast

By the time he was ready to sell *Abbey*, the starting gravity had been boosted to 1.059 (14.5 °P) and the beer finished about 1.016 (4 °P). He started adding sugar, using demerara that amounted to 3% of the extract, and later boosted that to help improve attenuation. "As I brewed it more, I realized that the (finishing gravity) needed to go lower," Lebesch said. "I still see (the need for more attenuation) in a lot of brewpub beers I taste, that maybe on the first tasting it is sweet. One of the hardest things to learn was making it easier to drink."

When he brewed the last 10-gallon test batch on his home-brewing system, Lebesch reduced the chocolate malt and thought he would recover color with additional caramel malt. When the color came in light, he ground up chocolate malt and did a mini-mash. Because his filter broke, he ended up with coarse grains in his serving kegs. "We took it to a tasting, and pretty soon somebody came up and told me, 'There are coffee grounds coming out of the tap.' "

Since taking charge of brewing operations at New Belgium in 1996, Peter Bouckaert has done little to change the *Abbey* recipe, although most often it is brewed as an all-malt beer. He continues to fine-tune fermentation. "We have a very robust yeast," he said. "I'm sure that if you compare it now with Chimay that it is very different. It has mutated." The yeast produces isoamyl acetate (the banana-fruity character Chimay is known for) in higher levels that Bouckaert would like. "We've changed the (fermentation) temperature, the pitching rate, trying to get it under control. There are always big variables," he said.

But nobody's spotted any coffee grounds.

From Mash Tun to Fermenter

When he wrote the book *Belgian Ale* (Brewers Publications, 1992), Pierre Rajotte billed sugar above malt in the chapter about fermentables. Given Americans' aversion in the early 1990s to brewing with sugar, that sent an important message. However, it would be a mistake to think that Trappist brewers don't put a higher priority on malt selection. Brother Thomas of Westmalle spoke often of the importance of choosing malts, making his decision based upon the character of each crop. Brewing director Jean-Marie Rock still selects Orval's malts after tasting samples of the latest barley crop.

These beers begin with a strong base, usually Pilsener malt, then, depending on the style, may include some pale malt for subtle complexity, one or two darker malts, and one or two types of sugar. Trappists use relatively simple recipes to create complex beers. In Chapter 8, we'll investigate the role of yeast in making that happen. This chapter begins with mashing essentials, water, and grain, before considering sugar, then includes just a few words about hops and spices. Certainly, sugar *is* important. Under Belgian law, beer can be made with up to 40% adjuncts—usually sugar, corn or wheat starch, or malt extract—and sugar contributes up 15 to 20% of fermentables in some of the best examples of these beers.

WATER

No standard water profile exists for brewing Trappist ales. As early as the thirteenth century, breweries in the territory that became Belgium began to locate beside sources of dependable brewing water, but dependable simply meant abundant and unpolluted. Brewing water wasn't a consideration in the 1800s, when today's Trappists rebuilt old monasteries or established new ones. Monastery brewers today speak with pride about the

Table 7.1 Trappist Water Profiles

Two Dutch homebrewers put together Belgian water profiles in the late 1990s. Jacques Bertens and Ronald Baert contacted Belgian water companies and compiled information from more than one hundred pumping stations. These profiles are based on averages within the region near the breweries. Most monastery breweries have their own water source, but it won't be much different than the water of the region.

	Calcium	Bicarbonate	Magnesium	Sodium	Sulfate	Chloride
Westmalle	41	91	8	16	62	26
Orval	96	287	4	5	25	13
Rochefort	82	240	10	6	32	17
Chimay	70	216	7	7	21	21
Achel	64	157	7	12	28	24
Westvleteren	114	370	10	125	145	139

Data courtesy of Jacques Bertens and Ronald Baert, listed in ppm (mg/L).

quality of their water, but when they use the word "purity," they don't mean mineral-free. For instance, Orval thought so much of the water from Mathilda Spring that the abbey considered bottling water instead of selling beer, yet the water is high in bicarbonate.

Westvleteren has the most extreme water—undoubtedly, one of the reasons that its beers once were known for a sour edge—and the monks choose to keep how they treat the water and its brewing profile a secret. Nearby Brouwerij Sint-Bernardus takes its water from a 130-meter-deep well, disinfects it, and notes it retains a high level of salt.

Orval and Rochefort must adjust for water that is slightly to moderately high in bicarbonate. At Rochefort, where the pH of brewing water is 7, mashing drops it to 5.8 to 5.9, and mineral acid in the kettle to 5.2. Many Belgian brewers use food-grade acid to lower pH.

For the most part, American commercial breweries don't treat water used in Belgian styles differently than they do in brewing other styles. That means removing chlorine and often making additions to adjust pH, particularly on the lighter beers. John Kimmich at the Alchemist Pub & Brewery in Vermont is an exception. He'll soften his water with magnesium sulfate for spicier, softer Belgian ales, and harden it with calcium sulfate for hoppier beers.

GRAIN AND MASHING

Recall that Brother Pierre of Rochefort once said, "Every brewer with some experience is able to copy our beers perfectly." Rochefort and other Trappists brew with malt from Mouterij Dingemans, and the Belgian malt is also available in the United

Brasserie Caracole puts its ingredients on display at the brewery (it has since discontinued using whole hops).

States. So must you use Dingemans malts, or at least another continental base malt, and a step mash like Rochefort?

"The differences are not night and day," said Ron Ryan of Cargill Malt–Specialty Products Group, which sells Dingemans in the United States. "If I were making a Belgian style, and I could afford it, then I would certainly consider them. There's no doubt European barleys have some advantages. They are plump, and you get great runoff."

Homebrewers can buy most of the malts available to professional brewers, including Dingemans and Malterie du Château (sold as Castle in the United States) from Belgium. Malterie du Château does its own malting for Pilsener and pale malts, but Dingemans produces its specialty malts, packaging them in Malterie du Château bags. Many brewers use some or all of the Weyermann malts from Germany or Franco-Belges from France to make Belgian styles, and several smaller brewers have won medals in major competitions using British malts.

With Pilsener malt at the heart of their beers, all the Trappist breweries conduct a step mash, as do many other producers of abbey ales. The number of rests, resting temperatures, and time at each stop may vary by a small measure (you'll find those that monastery breweries were willing to reveal in Chapter 2). The mash at Brewery Ommegang in New York would fit right in. Ommegang begins at 113° F (45° C) for 15 minutes, is raised to 144° F (62° C) for 35 minutes, then 158° F (70° C) for 25 minutes, and 172° F (78° C) for 5 minutes. This differs little from to the regimen suggested by Belgian brewing scientist Jean De Clerck, who played such an important role in Trappist brewing history, in his classic *A Textbook of Brewing*.

Ryan said a brewer limited to single-infusion can do just fine using the same Belgian malts. "Almost every malt sold in North America is well modified," he said. "If not, it is very hard to make beer with it. If you want well-attenuated beer, then do a long conversion about 146° F (63° C). You don't mash off hot, never let it get over 163° F (73° C), and you're not really going to end conversion. You'll be converting all the way into the kettle, until you denature."

Todd Ashman of Brewers Supply Group argues for tradition. "If you use an upward infusion, you'll create some interesting malt flavors," he said. "More like what the Trappists were using back in the day." Like Ryan, Ashman is a former brewer now working for a company that sells both imported and domestic malts. Ashman has made several trips to Belgium and is devoted to the full range of styles.

"There's a flavor there. A lot of it is growing varieties, some of it is the conditions," he said, referring to the barley. "I think it could also be the water they use in the malting process." In Belgium brewers often talk about the variety of barley used to produce their malt. Dingemans creates its Pilsener malt with

French-grown Optic, which is more expensive because it is free of pesticides used on other barleys and must be stored cold.

Continental and domestic malts differ in another way, too. North American malts are higher in soluble protein, which results in an excess level of free amino acids (FAN) in all-malt beers. However, because Belgian-style beers often contain 15 to 20% sugar, and may include other adjuncts, and adjuncts dilute FAN, brewers may decide to boost FAN by using at least some domestic base malt. "The effect is not so drastic that it's a deal breaker in either case," Ryan said. "The primary problem with high levels of FAN in finished beer is an increase in beer pH. It may actually be advantageous for bottle-conditioning to have some extra FAN around for a quick snack for the bottle-conditioning yeast. Like most brewing issues, it's all about balancing a number of conflicting factors to achieve the best result."

Lautering lasts about two hours at most Trappist breweries, often through a grant (this is Rochefort's). Duvel no longer uses a grant, because it can add color to beer.

SPECIALTY GRAINS AND SUGAR

In his book *Farmhouse Ales*, Phil Markowski writes that when small breweries make *bière de garde*, "handling multiple varieties of specialty malt is ... the norm. The small brewer is more likely to produce a more assertive product with an additional complexity of flavor not found in most large-scale breweries."[1] The relationship between complex grain bills and complex beers

Keeping It Simple

Phil Markowski made *Rochefort 10* and *St. Bernardus Abt 12* the reference beers when he first brewed his *Abbot 12*. "I tend to prefer their cleaner yeast character, as opposed to *Westvleteren 12* with its more pronounced 'burnt banana peel' and rubbery aromatics," he said. "I like a blend of banana malt and spices (from the yeast, that is) in a Trappist/abbey-style brew."

He intended *Abbot 12* to hold up to years of aging, as well as to be approachable upon release. "I wanted a moderate level of attenuation to leave sufficient residual sugars to balance the high alcohol content," he said. "I wanted that classic 'rummy' dark candi sugar character, so I used a good amount of dark candi sugar (as well as white sugar) to achieve that flavor." He adds hops only for bittering. (*Recipe on next page.*)

Southampton Abbot 12 with Rochefort 10, an inspiration for the American beer.

---

[1] Markowski, *Farmhouse Ales: Culture and Craftmanship in the Belgian Tradition* (Boulder, Colo.: Brewers Publications, 2004), 79.

Southampton Abbot 12

Original Gravity: 1.096 (23 °P)

Alcohol by Volume: 9.9%

Apparent Degree of Attenuation: 78%

IBU: 22

Malts: 2-row pale, Pilsener, Special "B"

Adjuncts: Sucrose, dark candi sugar (rocks)

Hops: German Perle, Styrian Goldings

Yeast: Proprietary strain

Primary Fermentation: 74 to 76° F (23 to 24.5° C)

Secondary: 2 weeks at 2° C

Also Noteworthy: Filtered, re-yeasted, cork-finished, and bottle-conditioned. Conditioned 4 weeks at 68 to 72° F (20 to 22° C)

does not extrapolate to Trappist breweries, as reflected in the rather uncomplicated recipe for Markowski's *Southampton Publick House Abbot 12*. Such simplicity sets him apart from most American brewers, commercial and amateur.

With such a wide range of flavorful malts, temptation sometimes gets the better of moderation. Here's a quick overview of the choices, in this case based on Belgian-kilned malts, although many brewers do just as well with American and British products with similar specifications:

Kilned malts

Munich and Aromatic: Munich (4 to 7 °L) adds maltiness and color, Aromatic (17-21 °L), a.k.a. melanoidin, adds an even stronger malt aroma and deeper color (a little aromatic goes a long way).

Roasted malts

Biscuit: As its name implies, adds a biscuity or bready quality. 18 to 27 °L.

Chocolate: Although tasting notes for abbey beers may use the word "chocolate," among the Trappists only Achel uses this roasted malt (300 to 380 °L). Adds aroma, deep red color, and nutty flavors when used in moderation, but can contribute a roastiness uncharacteristic for the style.

Caramel or crystal malts

These malts are stewed before kilning, converting the starch to sugars and creating a glasslike texture. Similarly colored malts from different suppliers may produce dramatically different flavors and aromas.

CaraVienna: Provides caramel-sweet aroma and flavor, deep amber color, and often a subtle, elegant finish. 19 to 27 °L.

CaraMunich: More robust than CaraVienna, with richer caramel-sweet aroma and more intense color, adding impression of plums, other dark fruits. 40 to 60 °L.

Special "B": Darkest of the Belgian crystal malts, richer still with caramel, adds to body and color, as well as the trademark raisinlike flavors in abbey beers, plus some toasted notes. 115 to 155 °L.

Ron Jeffries of Jolly Pumpkin Artisan Ales in Dexter, Michigan, speaks bluntly about the importance of not confusing a catalog of options with a recipe. "I think a lot of people make assumptions about the malts they are supposed to use that are just wrong," he said. "They tend to overuse them. The problem is, you see a list of malts that might be used, and some people think they have to use every one."

Jeffries understands why, and explains by discussing grain selection in his *Maracaibo Especial,* a dubbel-like winter seasonal. "I know this is going to be a well-attenuated beer, so I use some darker crystal to give that illusion of body, so it appears that the beer is much richer than you'd imagine," he said. Jeffries uses a 140 °L British crystal malt, because he believes it produces a rich caramel flavor as the beer matures. He tastes roasty, burnt flavors he doesn't like in the popular Belgian Special "B" malt.

He understands that most Trappists don't include a crystal malt that dark in their recipes. "I don't have access to those same sugars they do," he said. "I want to create those same flavors with malt."

Other brewers echo the thought. "You don't always have to start with the actual ingredients," said Tomme Arthur of Pizza Port in Solana Beach, California. "Think about candi sugar (dark rocks). There's a flavor you are looking for." He wasn't copying any Belgian brewer when he decided to caramelize raisins to use in his *SPF 8 Spring Saison* as well as his dubbel, At Allagash Brewing, Rob Tod couldn't find a source for dark candi sugar (rocks) when he first decided to brew a dubbel, so he used light-colored rock candy from a Connecticut company and counted on malt to add color and complexity.

Not every Belgian brewery uses sugar; Brasserie des Rocs, for one, points with pride to the fact that its beers are all malt. Its flagship, *Abbaye des Rocs,* certainly contradicts the idea of simple recipes, using seven malts and unspecified spices, proof that brewers must find their own balance. "You have to be careful

Sugar Basics

To boost alcohol, fermentability, and produce what Belgians refer to as a "more digestible" beer, plain sucrose—the stuff you can buy at your local grocery store—works just as well as clear candi sugar (rocks). The dark, rummy character that comes from caramelized sugar is harder to duplicate, and certainly not by using American brown sugar. Here is a quick sugar primer:

Candi sugar: References to "candi sugar" when Belgian brewers began using such an ingredient most often described caramel syrup, not the clear to dark rocks sold in the United States as "Belgian candi sugar." The rocks you liquefy by tossing into a kettle are made by lowering cotton strings with seed crystals into hot solutions of sugar. What we really care about is the sugar itself.

Today, when brewers at Westmalle and Orval refer to candi sugar, they specify using it in liquid form. Most other brewers, Trappist and secular, who once used "clear candi sugar" have replaced it with sucrose or dextrose. As well as adding white sugar to the kettle, Rochefort includes *cassonade brune* in its recipes. While that translates to "brown sugar," Candico in Antwerp produces something much different than Americans think of in making "candysugar" (its term) and *cassonade brune*: "granulated crystals, obtained from cooling down strongly concentrated sucrose-solutions boiled at very high temperatures." Most of Candico's sales to confectionary producers, biscuit factories, and breweries are "candysugar" in syrup form.

Sucrose: The basic white sugar you buy at A&P comes from sugar beets or sugar cane; both produce the same end product. They are crushed, dissolved in water, and the raw syrup is boiled down to concentrate it to a point where some fraction crystallizes. The remaining syrup is separated from what is now 95% pure sugar. The crystals are further processed several times to increase its purity, eventually yielding pure white crystals.

Sugar Basics, continued

Brown sugar: To produce brown sugar in North America, the crystals are left much smaller than for white sugar, and the syrup or molasses is not washed off completely. Many producers have in fact instituted processes in which they make brown sugars by blending refined white crystal sugar with molasses.

Dextrose: The "righthand" version of glucose, a monosaccharide derived from converted starches, much as what happens when mashing malted grain. Dextrose can be made from a variety of cheap sources, including corn, wheat, rice, and potatoes. Belgian brewers used glucose by the nineteenth century.

Invert sugar: Glucose and fructose together make up sucrose. When fructose is "inverted" by hydrolysis, the resulting invert sugar is theoretically easier for yeast to ferment.

Caramelized sugar: Caramelization occurs when a sugar molecule is heated to a high-enough temperature to begin to break down and create the characteristic flavors of caramel.

Sugar producers are extremely careful not to subject sugars to temperatures high enough to cause caramelization, because it would introduce these flavors and cause product loss (any sugar that is caramelized is no longer sugar, so it can't be crystallized). Caramel syrups are sold in Europe, giving brewers a variety of choices not available in the United States. Many American brewers use dark candi (rocks) as a substitute, but while the darkest provide a rummy, unrefined character, they don't come close to replicating the caramelized flavors found in darker Belgian ales.

As an alternative, you can make your own syrup. Randy Mosher provides a how-to in *Radical Brewing*, which he has since refined. His new instructions:

"Start with a bottle of plain corn syrup (Karo) in a heavy saucepan, and add to it 9 grams of ammonium bicarbonate, an ingredient that is sold as a sort of leavening in Middle Eastern specialty markets. (Ammonium phosphate, sold as a yeast nutrient, will also work.)

Sugar Basics, continued

Stir to dissolve. Cook over medium-high heat. In several minutes the sugar will start to darken. You can sample as you go, by removing a drop now and then and cooling it on aluminum foil, and tasting it when it is *well cooled*. When the desired color/flavor is reached, remove the pan from the heat, and *carefully* add cold water to create a thick syrup, which will be easy to add to your kettle.

This process creates class IV caramel, which is stable in beer pH and alcohol levels."

Mosher also suggests experimenting with a variety of unrefined sugars. If your goal is to clone a favorite Belgian beer, you may not venture there, although partially refined sugars were widely used in brewing one hundred years ago.[2]

[2] If you want to see what sort of magic Belgian yeasts might produce from wort made with a less traditional sugar, then start reading on p. 196 of *Radical Brewing*.

you don't get a specialty malt soup," Jeffries said. Todd Ashman agreed: "If you start to use these in excess, then they can pick up their own phenolics."

Most Belgian brewers avoid the problem by using sugar, sometimes sugar caramelized into a dark syrup, to add complexity and avoid malt overload. For American brewers, that takes getting used to.

"There used to be that feeling, back in our homebrew days, that sugar would leave you with a cidery beer," said Mark Ruedrich of North Coast Brewing. "We're not afraid of it anymore." If step one is getting over the fear of sugar, step two is learning to use enough.

Phil Markowski believes Americans still shy away from sugar for another reason. "I think that one of the main areas that differentiate American versions of Belgian ales from the classic (Belgian) versions is attenuation," he said. "I believe that there is still a fairly prevalent anti-adjunct bias among many American brewers, both amateur and professional, that makes them hold back from using enough sugar to achieve the same level of dryness that the classic Belgian examples exhibit. It seems that many of these brewers tend to think of adjuncts as 'dishonest' ingredients. Until one embraces the use of notable amounts of sugar adjuncts in replicating classic Trappist-abbey styles, they will fall short of the mark."

Those Belgian brewers who will discuss what percentage of fermentables comes from sugar put it at between 15 and 20%. "I know of breweries in Belgium that use up to 30% glucose as a portion of their extract," said Randy Thiel of Brewery Ommegang. He said concerns about inhibiting yeast metabolism are unfounded.

After Victory Brewing Company in Downingtown, Pennsylvania, began brewing *Golden Monkey*, a tripel, co-owner/brewer Ron Barchet sent samples of clear candi sugar (rocks) to Archer Daniels Midland to see what sort of similar product the food processing giant could provide. "We didn't want to be spending $2 a pound for sugar, so we asked them give us an analysis," he said. "They told us it looks just like reconstituted sugar, and that if we wanted to match it not to buy anything from them. Buy sugar."

Professional brewers and most homebrewers may find it easier just to spend the money and use the product called dark candi sugar. Barchet, who buys this for Victory's *V-Twelve*, was particularly interested to hear about a friend of mine who had begun to experiment with making his own caramelized sugar. "Start with the idea that the spirit of Belgium is to make a great beer with what we have," he said. "Then, it is almost anti-spirit to spend $2 a pound for candi sugar. The Belgians would have asked, 'What is the cheapest sugar I have?' and that was local sugar."

HOPS AND SPICES

Spencer Tracy once offered very basic advice about acting: "Know your lines and don't bump into the furniture." Belgian brewers expect much the same of their hops. They take pride in quality ingredients, but in most cases, the hops should supplement malt and fermentation character in Trappist or abbey-style beers rather than calling attention to themselves. Trappist beer usually have a BU:GU ratio of less than 1:2, often quite a bit less.[3] Some breweries use only a bittering addition. When they include hops for aroma, they choose noble varieties.

We can find exceptions. *Cuvée de l'Ermitage* from the Union Brewery (brewer of Grimbergen and other beers) once was noted for its hop flavor and dry finish, although today it is noticeably sweeter. The De Ranke brewery dry hops *Guldenberg*, a tripel, making it refreshingly bitter. Among Trappist beers, you won't miss the hops in *Orval*, *Westvleteren Blond*, or *Westmalle Tripel* and *Extra*.

Although Chimay has long used a Northwest American hop for its bittering charge, other Trappists brew with hops from the Continent, favoring those lower in alpha acids for

---

[3] The "BU:GU (hops to gravity) ratio" was, to the best of my knowledge, created by Ray Daniels for *Designing Great Beers*, and represents IBUs divided by gravity units.

both bittering and flavor. Styrian Goldings, Hallertau, and Saaz top the list. While many brewers try to include at least a measure of Belgian hops, production continues to dwindle within Belgium itself. Belgian brokers usually offer hops from Germany, Slovenia, and the Czech Republic, with some British products included.

Trappist brewers basically don't use spices, nor do the larger brewers producing abbey-type beers. Rochefort includes a bit of coriander in its beers, while Chimay spices only *Dorée*, the monks' beer.

Of course, plenty of spiced dubbels, tripels, and dark strongs exist. These beers capture awards in international competitions … and purists hate them. You wouldn't call the examples traditional, but they are part of the present and could be more of the future. Even those of us who would rather let yeast add spicy character in these styles must admit that spicing done well can complement yeast characteristics. However, if a drinker can name the spices, it's a sign they are overdone.[4]

---

[4] Before you start using spices, consider the big picture, starting on p. 158 of *Radical Brewing.*

Brother Jos (above) stands at the stainless steel mash tun in Westvleteren's brewhouse. Silence seems natural in the hallways of the abbey (right).

Steam rises from the brewery at Orval, built in classic style with the brewhouse on the second floor.

Beer cafés take particular pride in offering Trappist beers. This one in Ghent serves Westmalle Dubbel on tap.

This beer wagon (above) parked in the courtyard at Brouwerij Kerkom no longer makes deliveries. Brewer Marc Limet emphasizes beer must be "digestible" and enjoys his own along with a meal at Het Vijgeblad in Beringen.

Rochefort's brewhouse has been described as the "Cathedral of Beer." The mash tun looms above, and the brewing kettle in the foreground is no longer used.

A white cross hangs in the background behind two copper kettles at Westmalle.

The message means "Quiet … here matures the Trappist," and the much-loved Westvleteren 12 spends up to ten weeks in the horizontal lagering tanks in the cellar below.

The idea for the inscription at Westvleteren was taken from Duvel Moortgat, where a sign on its warehouse admonishes drivers not to disturb "den Duvel." Here, a turnabout in Breendonk makes it clear Duvel Moortgat is nearby.

Equipment (above) from early in the twentieth century sits in a cellar hallway that Rochefort formerly used to bottle-condition its beer. Below, the mill at Brasserie Caracole (left) is a working antique, while Brouwerij Het Anker has retired some antiques (right), using them to decorate the area outside the hotel it operates in space once occupied by the brewery.

Brasserie Caracole claims to operate the last wood-fired kettles (set in brick) in Europe.

Orval uses a grant during lautering, which takes three hours.

A lay worker at Westmalle (above) top crops yeast. The brewery installed a state-of-the-art bottling line (below) in 1999.

eight

Yeast and Fermentation

*B*rewers no longer must culture yeast from the dregs of Belgian bottles in order to brew with Belgian yeast, as Jeff Lebesch did in fermenting his test batches of *New Belgium Abbey*. Any of the four primary yeasts (remember, three breweries use yeast from Westmalle) employed by the Trappists can be acquired from American vendors, albeit versions not exactly like the originals. Many other yeasts from Belgian breweries, including Duvel Moortgat, also are available.

Starting with the right stuff could hardly be easier. Handling fermentation like a monk remains the challenge.

Nobody has come up with a formula that tells you if you pitch X amount of yeast into a beer with an initial gravity of Y, you can ferment it at Z temperature and produce a perfect beer. "Brewing is a compromise," said Peter Bouckaert of New Belgium Brewing. "You have to take into account so many factors. You can't look at the temperature as a sole factor. It's an interaction. You need to see any beer you create as a holistic thing."

This chapter examines the tradeoffs involved in maximizing the yeast-driven flavors that set Trappist beers and their offspring

Table 8.1 White Labs Belgian Yeast Descriptions

White Labs Strain Number	WLP500	WLP510	WLP530	WLP550	WLP570
Flocculation	Low	Medium	Medium-High	Medium	Low
Attenuation %	Medium-High	Medium-High	Medium-High	High	Medium
Temperature Range and Resulting Flavor Profiles High (75-85° F) (24-29° C)	Fruity / Mod. Phenolic / Solvent	Spicy / Acidic / Solvent	Spicy / Phenolic / Solvent	Earthy / Phenolic / Solvent	Fruity / Mod. Phenolic / Sulfur
Medium (67-75° F) (19-24° C)	Spicy / Light Phenol / Fruity	Spicy / Acidic / Clean	Spicy / Light Phenol / Fruity	Fruity / Phenolic / Sulfur	Fruity / Phenolic / Sulfur
Low (58-66° F) (14-19° C)	Clean / Balanced / Earthy	Clean / Crisp / Light Phenol	Peppery / Spicy / Light Phenol	Clean / Light Phenol / Spicy	Phenolic / Spicy

About Attenuation: Low   Less than 70%

                 Medium   70-80%

                 High   80-90%

apart while minimizing undesirable characteristics that are closely linked. We'll discuss esters and higher alcohols, what sets Belgian yeast apart from other *Saccharomyces cerevisiae*, fermentation temperatures, pitching rates, and the role of fermenter geometry.

White Labs and Wyeast, the largest yeast suppliers for the craftbrewing and homebrewing communities, provided tables for this chapter that include not only the information you usually see about their yeast (such as possible attenuation) but also flavor characteristics they expect their yeasts to produce with standard pitching rates and oxygenation levels.

Certain yeast characteristics shouldn't be taken for granted. We understand all yeasts produce diacetyl, DMS (dimethyl sulfide), acetaldehyde, and other by-products that may not be desirable in finished beer. So, good basic fermentation practices can't be suspended when it comes to working with these yeasts. Meanwhile, we anticipate that Belgian yeasts will attenuate well and be alcohol tolerant, accepting the fact that many do not flocculate that well, requiring filtering or longer lagering.

After we get those basics out of the way, we can focus on flavor. Esters, phenols, and higher alcohols deliver the fruity, spicy, complex aromas and flavors that set Belgian strong ales apart. Pears, apples, tangerines, oranges, and strawberries may all be detected, with raisins, plums, figs, and prunes in beers that include darker malts and/or sugars. We also expect peppery, perfumy, and roselike characteristics.

ESTERS AND HIGHER ALCOHOLS

Esters constitute the most important aroma compounds in beer. They make up the largest family of beer aroma compounds, and in general impart a fruity character. Most are desirable, but not the relatively common ethyl acetate (solventy, like nail polish remover) and not necessarily isoamyl acetate (banana, fruity).

Higher alcohols represent the fusel alcohols produced during primary fermentation in addition to ethanol. They contribute harsh solventlike flavors when not converted to softer esters during secondary fermentation. However, higher alcohols may also increase the complexity of a beer, and those that soften in secondary add spicy, perfumy, and roselike aromas.

Most of the studies about the formation of esters and higher alcohols, and the relationship between the two, have focused on lager beers, for the simple reason that most beer produced worldwide is lager. Fortunately, some of that research is relative to fermenting ales.

"My belief is that, directionally, many of the findings with lager beer would be applicable to ale—unlike other flavor categories (such as sulfur compounds) where there are significant differences in gene expression or capability between ale and lager yeast," said Gregory Casey, director of brewing services at Coors Brewing Company. "In the case of esters and higher alcohols, the pathways leading to their formation are 'core' pathways for *Saccharomyces* yeasts in general."

Casey presented his findings at the 2005 Rocky Mountain Microbrewing Symposium. He concluded that:

- Higher alcohol production by yeast is directly correlated with the amount of yeast growth during fermentation. Yeast growth depends on another set of relationships, including original gravity, fermentation temperature, and pitching rate.

- Ester production by yeast is inversely related to yeast growth. This relationship can be uncoupled by key process variables, especially trub and fermenter design.

Casey also cited a study that found that temperature had a much greater effect on ester production than pitching rate; increased pitching rates lowered ethyl acetate levels; and increased temperature increased ethyl acetate levels.

Tradeoffs: Most esters are desirable, some higher alcohols may be. Yeast growth promotes higher alcohol production and inhibits ester production.

BELGIAN YEAST STRAINS

Even though Belgians did not brew beers as strong or nearly as well attenuated at the beginning of the twentieth century, G.M. Johnson documented the strength of Belgian yeasts in a paper written in 1895:

"It is also a curious fact that with these worts such a thing as yeast weakness is unknown. Notwithstanding the fact that the attenuation of the wort does not generally exceed 66%, about 15 kilos of yeast are produced to the 100 of malt mashed. … In England much less is produced. That this yeast is very strong is also a fact. Belgian distillers know it well, as speed in fermentation is one of their objects; they find that wash pitched with Belgian yeast will produce considerably more alcohol in the first twenty-four hours than English yeast."[1]

Belgian yeast strains *are* different. We think in terms of results; they tolerate higher alcohols, attenuate well, and generate a range of phenolics and esters. Chris White of White Labs

[1] Johnson, "Brewing in Belgium and Belgian Beers": *Journal of the Federated Institutes of Brewing* (1895): 462.

Table 8.2 Wyeast Laboratories Belgian Yeast Flavor Profile Descriptions

Wyeast Strain Number	1214	1388	1762	3522	3787	3538	3864
Flocculation	Medium	Low	Medium	High	Medium	High	Medium
Attenuation %	72-76	65-75	73-77	72-76	75-80	75-78	75-79
Temperature Range 75° F-85° F (24-29° C) and Resulting Flavor Profiles	Clove	Alcohol	Solvent	Clove	Bubblegum	Bubblegum	Banana
	Bubblegum	Phenolic	Alcohol	Bubblegum	Clove	Solvent	Clove
	Banana	Fruity	Phenolic	Tart	Alcohol	Banana	Lt. Phenolic
	Alcohol	Tart		Phenolic	Fruity	Clove	Fruity
	Rose	Banana			Tart	Phenolic	
	Fruity				Lt. Solvent	Lt. Tart	
65 °F-75° F (18-24° C)	Clove	Lt. Fruity	Clean	Clean	Clove	Bubblegum	Fruity
	Alcohol	Alcohol	Lt. Fruity	Malty	Alcohol	Fruity	Lt. Clove
	Phenolic				Pineapple	Clove	Sulfur
	Fruity						

Notes to Brewers:

1. All of these descriptions are based on standard pitch rates, oxygenation levels, and brewing practices.

2. All of the listed flavor profiles can be changed by altering one of many factors other than temperature.

3. Alcohol tolerance is also affected by many factors, and the optimum can be achieved using proper pitch rates, oxygenation, and brewing practices.

looks at them under a microscope and sees cells that have a smaller surface area than other ale yeast. In studying the genetics, Dave Logsdon of Wyeast Laboratories found, "Belgian yeasts have a lot in common with wine yeasts. They have phenolic compounds that are similar to wine yeasts."

Name That Yeast

Chapters 2 through 5 of this book provided information about which breweries bottle with their primary yeast. If you have the tools and experience, you might want to culture yeast from bottled beer to ferment your beers. However, be aware that the yeast you'll get from bottled beer has already been through a demanding battle. "We could never take a yeast from the bottle," said Chris White of White Labs.

Fermenting these styles presents enough variables that it can be reassuring to eliminate one—that is, the viability of the yeast you are starting with. Breweries routinely turn to a new starter after pitching a certain number of generations, and homebrewers can enjoy the same benefit by buying yeast already cleaned up and checked by pros before it goes out the door.

Additionally, if you really want yeast from a particular Trappist brewery, a commercial version already exists. Granted, you can't expect them to act like yeast freshly cropped from a Trappist fermentation. That's one reason yeast suppliers use numbers to identify their products, rather than listing the source brewery. Left on their own, yeast strains change over time. So, while Wyeast may have kept its 1214 much the same in the twenty years since it was taken from Chimay, Chimay's itself likely changed.

That said, you may adjust your fermentation schedule because you know that Wyeast 1762 originated at Rochefort, and we can study Rochefort's production process. Logsdon and White hear the "where did that yeast come from" question all the time. "We try to avoid referring

Name That Yeast, continued

to them (by source), but that is what everybody wants to know," White said. That's why we're listing the sources here.

Before you start, think about what Vinnie Cilurzo of Russian River Brewing said when talking about White Labs WLP500 (Trappist Ale). "People are enamored with the idea this is Chimay yeast. I try not to think that way," he said. "*Chimay* doesn't have nearly the fruit that you get from the (WLP500) yeast. There are a lot of dynamics that go into the flavor you get at the end."

Wyeast sources: 1214 (Chimay), 1762 (Rochefort), 3522 (Achouffe), 3787 (Westmalle), 3864 (Unibroue), 1388 (Duvel), 3538 (Corsendonk-Bocq).

White Labs sources: WLP500 (Chimay), WLP510 (Orval), WLP530 (Westmalle), WLP540 (Rochefort), WLP550 (Achouffe), WLP570 (Duvel).

Wyeast and White Labs both continue to add to what they offer. White Labs rolled out a blend (WLP575) early in 2005, which was too new for our tables. It combines two Trappist ale yeast strains and one Belgian ale yeast strain. "We wanted to lower the fruitiness and get it drier without too much manipulation on the part of the brewer," White said. In other words, all other conditions being equal, WLP575 will produce a beer less fruity, exhibiting less banana character, than the yeast White calls "Trappist" (WLP500). White has long advocated that brewers blend yeast for complexity, and spent about a year and a half experimenting with WLP575.

When yeast strains merge, one may grow dominant in subsequent generations. White recommends using the blend for about five generations. "When we go to ten, we definitely start to see population changes," he said. "But the flavor characteristics are still there. It depends on how much consistency you are after."

Belgian yeasts also share characteristics with several wheat yeasts, although the desirable phenolics we expect in Belgian beers are decidedly different than clovelike phenolics common in Bavarian wheat beers. In 2003 Wyeast and Microanalytics Corporation tested a variety of wheat and Belgian yeast strains with a gas chromatograph. They designed the experiments to measure the extent and concentration of various aroma compounds produced by different yeast strains. Logsdon and Larry Nielsen of Microanalytics presented their findings at the 2003 Craft Brewers Conference.

Malted and unmalted wheat made up about 40% of the grist of the 1.058 (14.3 °P) base beer, so results with higher-gravity barley-based worts including sugar (which makes ester profiles more intense) would change. When interacting with wheat in the grist, Wyeast 1214, 3787, and 3522 all registered higher levels of 4-vinyl guaiacol, which adds clove flavor, than German and Bavarian Wheat yeasts. The panel identified them as spicy, and singled out the clove in 1214 and 3522. One the other hand, Wyeast 1762 showed only trace amounts, and the panel identified no clove or spice characteristics. Wyeast 1214, 3787, and 3522 also produced wheat-yeast-like concentrations of styrene, which has a resiny flavor perceived as phenolic by some. Again, Wyeast 1762 had only trace amounts. In contrast, Wyeast 1762 registered levels of phenyl ethyl alcohol and phenyl ethyl acetate (rose and honey) closer to the other Belgian strains. Phenyl ethyl alcohol is necessary for the recognized flavor of beer, and may stand out more in beers fermented with 1762 because of lower levels of clove and spices.

White Labs acquired gas chromatography equipment at the beginning of 2005, and should eventually be able to assemble interesting data about ester and fusel production based upon variations in temperature and in open fermentation versus closed. AleSmith Brewing Company of San Diego expanded its brewery in 2005, supplementing open fermenters with closed. AleSmith previously fermented Belgian beers at very warm temperatures, and could provide valuable side-by-side data.

White suggests that homebrewers needn't wait for those results. "I think homebrewers would do best by sensory analysis, with side-by-side fermentations," he said. In 2001 the Great Northern Brewers Club of Anchorage, Alaska, conducted an experiment in fermenting tripels with yeast as the variable. Club members brewed a 1-barrel batch and split the wort into six carboys, adding different yeast to each one, then fermenting and conditioning them identically. The brewers collected empirical data along the way, then tasted the finished beers blind. All beers fermented for eighteen days at 70 to 75° F (21 to 24° C), which was not necessarily ideal for some of the yeast. Beers spent more than three more months conditioning and lagering.

Wyeast 1056 (American Ale Yeast) acted as the control yeast, and working in a wort rich with candi sugar (more than 10%) and at a higher fermentation temperature than usual had a stunning apparent attenuation of 87.8%. The 1056 beer finished last in sensory evaluations, not surprisingly lacking in Belgian characteristics. The group found, "Alcohol overwhelms all other flavors, finishing dry and harsh. Minor modifications to the recipe and lower fermentation temperatures would have produced a nice blonde barley wine."

The two yeasts not widely available, Brewtek CL-320 and CL-300, rated highest in sensory tests. The Brewing-Science Institute in Colorado (*www.brewingscience.com*) sells them to homebrewers on plates and to commercial breweries in pitchable quantities. Both earned praise for their complexity and low production of higher alcohols.

Somewhat surprisingly, neither Wyeast 3787 nor Wyeast 1762 attenuated nearly as well as they do in the Belgian breweries from which they came, or at several American commercial breweries that use the strains. The results simply confirm the importance of treating each of these yeasts individually when considering everything from pitching rates to fermentation temperature.[2]

When Wyeast and White Labs provide guidelines for apparent attenuation, they base them on all-malt beers, usually not fermented at the top of the suggested temperature range. Beers with sugar providing more than 10% of their fermentables will attenuate further, and further still at higher temperatures. "It's really important that brewers let them reach terminal gravity," Logsdon said. "I have heard too many brewers who say 'I'm going to stop it here,' because they've calculated what the attenuation should be. The worst thing you can do is get incomplete fermentation."

Tradeoffs: Higher original gravity produces more esters, as does higher attenuation. More aeration lowers ester production. Belgian yeasts naturally produce more esters, including some related to wheat yeasts. Logsdon notes, "Fusel alcohol raises perception of isoamyl acetate. It wasn't detected as strongly when fusels were lower."

FERMENTATION TEMPERATURES

Yeast producers offer suggested fermentation temperatures that might be considered fail-safe that are lower than many

[2] Dennis Urban and Mark Staples, "Great Northern Brewers' Trippel Yeast Experiment," *Zymurgy* 24:6 (November-December 2001): 50-52+.

Belgian brewers reach. The companies don't want to see brewers, enchanted by reports of high temperatures at which *some* Belgians ferment, pitching at the top of a range or above. "For homebrewers, the problem is lack of control," Logsdon said. "If they start at 75° F and let it go, then they are going to get lots of higher alcohol and solventy character," Logsdon said.

Once a yeast has gone over the top, professionals might not be able to save it. Brother Joris, who supervises brewing at Westvleteren, still gets up in the middle of the night if he fears a fermentation will zoom past 84° F (29° C). He knows if he doesn't slow the rise early enough and then tries to reduce the temperature, his yeast may crash. Others report White Labs WLP530 and Wyeast 3787, both Westmalle offspring, acting the same way for them. "When you cool them, they stop," White said. "They go into survival mode. You can try rousing them, raising the temperature, but they won't start again. You just have to add a new yeast. You don't want to let it spike, and that can be hard to control in a homebrew situation."

The flavor profiles offered here by White Labs and Wyeast provide a strong start toward thinking about the variables inv ed in working with these yeasts. It helps to recognize where in the fermentation cycle flavors are created. You get more phenolics (produced) at lower temperatures," White said. "The absence of esters makes them stand out more. If you continue to suppress the esters, then you will continue to perceive the phenolics. You are looking for a balance."

Russian River on the West Coast and Allagash on the East Coast found a similar balance through trial and error, with both eventually letting the temperature rise during the fermentation process, keeping the esters and attenuation they wanted without

One Yeast, Three Beers

Westmalle, Westvleteren, and Achel all ferment their beer with Westmalle yeast. Westvleteren and Achel pick up recently cropped yeast on the day they brew.

Achel	*Achel Bruin 8 (1.079–19 °P, 22 IBU)*
Yeast is pitched at 63 to 64° F (17 to 18° C) Top temperature 72 to 73° F (22 to 23° C) Fermentation in cylindro-conical tanks	Sweet and malty, a little like a chocolate milkshake, albeit one dosed with dark rum. Subdued aromas, plenty of malt flavor, well rounded.
Westmalle	*Westmalle Dubbel (1.063–15.6 °P, 24 IBU)*
Yeast is pitched at 64° F (18° C) Top temperature 68° F (20° C) Fermentation in closed squares	Cocoa nose, dry and complex. A bit sweet up front, rum giving way to dark fruit. Smooth to the end, although it finishes dry. An example of yeast deferring to malt and dark caramel syrup.
Westvleteren	*Westvleteren 8 (1.072–17.6 °P, 35 IBU)*
Yeast is pitched at 68° F (20° C) Top temperature 82 to 84° F (28 to 29° C) Open fermentation	A restaurant near us serves plantains in mole sauce. Scorch that a bit, and you have this beer (at about four months since bottling), with a first impression of burned chocolate and banana. Darker fruits, rum begin to appear at mid-palate. Finishes dry even when young; a complex beer that will improve with age.

getting solventy notes. "One of the things that starting cooler does, is it leaves some of the fatty acids for ester production otherwise utilized early by yeast growth," Logsdon said.

Tradeoffs: Increased temperature increases ethyl acetate levels, floral and fruity esters, and may be necessary for some of these yeasts to finish attenuating. Lower temperature restrains ester production, promotes perception of phenols.

PITCHING RATES

American microbreweries pitch at a "standard" rate of 1 million cells of yeast per milliliter of wort per degree Plato. For example, Brewery Ommegang pitches 18.5 million cells per milliliter for its 1.076 (18.5 °P) *Ommegang.*

In contrast, Moortgat in Belgium pitches just 7.5 million cells per milliliter for a beer with an original gravity of 16.9 °P (1.069). Orval pitches 10 million cells per milliliter for its 13.6 °P (1.055) *Orval,* and Rochefort pitches at a rate of 15 million cells per milliliter for all its beers, ranging from 17.5 °P to 23 °P (1.072 to 1.096). Those breweries settled on pitching levels that optimize flavor and aroma characteristics, although their rates are lower than conventional wisdom would predict. Of course, these beers contain a good percentage of sugar, simple sugars are easier for yeast to process, and the breweries are confident about the viability of their yeast.

Sometimes a brewer does well breaking the rules. One homebrewer submitting information for this book wrote, "I end up with a more interesting beer if I use less yeast, but the risk of a bad batch is too great."

White understands. "On the professional level, the norm is pitching 2 liters (of yeast) per barrel," he said. "Belgians are

Top Cropping

Dave Logsdon of Wyeast Laboratories suggests that the best time to top crop yeast arrives when apparent attenuation slips past 50%, "when the yeast head is near its maximum density, and prior to alcohol levels increasing beyond 5.25%. The yeast at this state has very high viability and is optimum for repitching immediately or soon after harvesting."

Ron Jeffries of Jolly Pumpkin Ales emphasized the importance of acquiring a feel for when yeast should be taken. "There's a local cheesemaker in Ann Arbor, he has all these molds," he said. "You ask him exactly what's going on, and he can't tell you. He learned 'how' rather than 'why.' So much of it is the feel and the look and the texture. The best thing is to do it, and do it again."

Because Jeffries pitches warm, and fermentation can be fast and furious, he often harvests yeast by the second day. "It should look like a rich lather, with a dense head on top," he said. "If you wait too long, it will have settled back in." When you are starting, be a little conservative, and leave enough yeast behind to finish the job. He uses sanitary plastic scoops to grab the yeast and stores it in sanitary plastic buckets.

below that. I've talked some (American) brewers into cutting back on their pitching level, and they are surprised their fermentations are stronger. By pitching a little less, if your yeast is healthy, flavor is going to be spit out during growth." He added a warning: "Of course, if you don't pitch enough, you get solventy. The Belgians know where that balance is."

Given that most homebrewers already underpitch, and the downside of underpitching, if you decide to try pitching at lower rates, treat it as an experiment.

Tradeoffs: Higher pitching rates lower ethyl acetate levels. Very high or very low pitching rates increase ester levels.

FERMENTER GEOMETRY

As with other brewing research, studies involving fermenter geometry have focused on lager beers. Ester production by yeast is inversely related to yeast growth, but research by Greg Casey at Coors has shown this relationship can be uncoupled by fermenter design. In simplest terms, when CO_2 levels increase around the yeast in a fermenter, the levels of ester production decrease. "A classic example of a design impact became apparent with the introduction of cylindro-conicals in replacement of traditional box fermenters," Casey said. "Due to the greater height-to-width ratio of the former, many of the early lagers coming out of cylindro-conicals were much less estery than the box-fermented counterpart (all other things being equal). This 'washed-out' ester character was linked to CO_2 inhibition, a finding which has since been applied in designing cylindro-conicals to more reasonable ratios (lower height to width)."

After Duvel Moortgat shifted fermentation from open rectangular tanks to cylindro-conicals, the concentration of isoamyl acetate dropped from about 3 to 4 milligrams per liter to 2 to 3 milligrams per liter. "That was good for our beer," said technical director Hedwig Neven. At Brewery Ommegang, Randy Thiel reported being similarly pleased with results from cylindro-conicals.

That doesn't mean cylindro-conical tanks suit every beer. That's why Orval and Rochefort moved carefully before adding c-c tanks, and why American brewers would like to know more when expanding. "There are a million questions about fermentation geometry, most of which are extremely

Golden Monkey

Original Gravity: 1.085 (20.4 °P)

Alcohol by Volume: 9.5%

Apparent Degree of Attenuation: 83%

IBU: 28 to 30

Malts: German Pilsener

Adjuncts: Sucrose

Spices: Coriander

Hops: Tettnang, Saaz

Yeast: Proprietary strain acquired in Belgium

Primary Fermentation: 68 to 70° F (20 to 21° C) 5-6 days

Secondary Fermentation: Slowly lowered to 30° F (-1° C), 2 to 5 weeks

Also Noteworthy: Refermentation in the bottle; sometimes kraeusened, other times with sugar and fresh yeast

difficult to determine what the real differences are," said Ron Ryan of Cargill.

Wl...ie added that brewers aren't alone. "The wine industry has the same question about tank configuration," he said. "I've been approached by some pretty good wine people about doing some research."

When Victory Brewing expanded in 2004 and 2005, Ron Barchet and Bill Covaleski erred on the side of caution, retaining shallow fermenters to use for *Golden Monkey*, their tripel, and other Belgian-style beers. "We moved it around, tried it in (a tank) that has a shallow cone, putting it in a lager tank," Barchet said. He preferred to keep *Golden Monkey* in a tank with a 1-to-1 ratio—"We like the height constraint, and we need to be able to get the yeast off the top"—but as *Golden Monkey* sales rose, he experimented with fermenting in a unitank with a height-to-width ratio of 1.8 to 1.

"We've had really good results by changing the temperature a bit," Barchet said. Attenuation remained the same or better, sometimes reaching 88%. More importantly, the beer fares well in sensory evaluation. "It really is a matter of flavor. That's what we're looking at, and we've been happy," he said.

Ron Jeffries at Jolly Pumpkin Ales votes for flat, open fermentation. His fermenters are not only open but shallow, with some twice as wide as deep and none with a height-to-width ratio above 1 to 1. "I really like open," he said. "To some people it sounds silly. I like the flavor better than the beer from conicals. Also, I think you can learn a lot from your yeast by watching it ferment. You get a better feeling for your yeast."

Jeffries talks like somebody who has gone into partnership with his yeast, rather than expecting it to follow his commands.

"I usually let (fermentation) start in the upper 60s and finish in the mid-80s. I try not to mess with it," he said. "For me, all the best beers I've made with Belgian yeast have been the ones I've done the least with. The yeast is almost always one step ahead of me. I've learned, don't slow them once they start. If you try (to dial down the temperature), what you think is under control isn't. Once the temperature jumps up, step back."

Tradeoffs: Horizontal tanks increase esters, while open fermentation lowers esters (because of additional contact with oxygen), and cylindro-conicals lower esters.

PUTTING IT TOGETHER

What does this all mean for a brewer, and particularly for a homebrewer? Although Belgian yeasts work at higher temperatures, you've still got to be able to control fermentation, and that begins with understanding the temperature of fermenting wort. It sounds basic, but the monks at Westvleteren don't measure the ambient temperature of their fermentation room but the wort in the heart of their open tanks. Few homebrewers have probes in their fermentation vessels. If they did they might be surprised. "At a minimum, you'd expect a temperature rise in moderate fermentation to be 7 degrees, and it might get a lot hotter," Logsdon said. "It's almost a given that homebrewers will undermeasure the temperature." A strip thermometer on the side of a glass carboy will be more accurate than measuring the ambient temperature, but glass is a good insulator.

Using multiple fermenters reduces the height-to-width ratio, increasing the amount of wort in contact with the air and possibly slowing temperature surges (if the surrounding air is cooler). "I'd go shallow, and I wouldn't even put an airlock on,"

White said. Using plastic buckets rather than glass carboys will make it easier to top crop yeast for use in another fermentation or bottling.

That's one example of finding a balance. Consider Logsdon talking about another. "Boosting pitching rate reduces esters and creates more acetaldehyde (green apple). Reducing aeration increases esters," he said. He paused, then laughed. "Everybody has a different opinion of optimal profile."

Now consider how one commercial brewer puts the science, and years of experience, to use. At the Pizza Port brewery in California, Tomme Arthur tried a variety of approaches before establishing a similar program for all his Belgian-style beers, including a dubbel. He notes that your mileage may vary:

"Currently, we are overpitching the cell count (don't ask by how much, I don't know). We are then undercutting our oxygen levels at knockout, forcing the yeast to create esters by going through a starved lag phase. We are now fermenting at 64° F (18° C) to start, at which point we cut the yeast loose and let the fermentation go. In other words, at this point we are not using the jackets on the fermenter to cool the beer. We typically see an increase of ferment temperature into the high 70s when we reach terminal gravity. This ramping-up process works great, as we get the yeast to finish in a higher temperature range, with much of the alcohol production taking place at lower temperatures, thereby minimizing fusel alcohol production. Spicy phenols are created initially, followed by much of the ester production as the beer ferments at a warmer temperature."

nine
Bottling

*J*ust as it takes a different mindset for a brewer who has learned British and German brewing techniques to successfully make Trappist and abbey beers, bottling requires thinking a little differently as well. This chapter examines how.

Only two Trappist beers—*Westmalle Dubbel* and *Chimay White*—are even served on draft. All the beers sold by the Trappists, and most of the best examples in this book, undergo refermentation in the bottle, reaching a surprisingly high level of carbonation after an extended period of warm conditioning and sometimes additional conditioning.

The process stands in contrast to bottle-conditioning homebrewed beers or bottling a few 22-ounce bottles for sale in a brewpub. "It's a constant headache," said Randy Thiel of Brewery Ommegang, which was built with a dedicated warm room. "But it adds complexity to the beer, and you need to do it to achieve carbonation you never could in a keg. When you pop the cork, and beer is foaming all over the place, and you pour it into a special glass, it's a ceremony. Us beer geeks are not afraid of that."

Old bottles and an old bottling device from Westvleteren are on display at In De Vrede.

Among Trappists and other breweries that practice refermentation in the bottle, what Westmalle does is fairly standard. Workers centrifuge much of the dead yeast from the wort before bottling begins, then dose it with sugar and fresh yeast before bottling. The *Dubbel* takes two weeks to condition at 70 to 73° F (21 to 23° C) in a temperature-controlled warm room, while the *Tripel* spends three weeks in underground cellars that hold 125,000 cases.

An American brewer needs a warm room (or closet) but not necessarily a centrifuge (or filter). Westvleteren neither centrifuges nor filters, relying instead on a long period of lagering to settle out the spent yeast.

In the United States commercial breweries take a range of approaches. At one end of the spectrum, Avery Brewing in Colorado does not bottle-condition ("I think bottle-conditioning is really hard," Adam Avery said. "I like brilliant beer."). At the other, after once bottle-conditioning some beer and force-carbonating others, Allagash in Maine recently began bottle-conditioning all its abbey-style beers.

At Victory Brewing in Pennsylvania, "We prefer to use kraeusen," said Ron Barchet. "If we can't, then we'll use invert sugar and fresh yeast." In the winter Victory kraeusens *Golden Monkey* with lager yeast rather than the stronger yeast it is brewed with, because the warm room isn't really a warm room, but a space (subject to changes in ambient temperature) dedicated to conditioning. Barchet says they haven't noticed a difference.

When homebrewers ask Allagash founder Rob Tod about bottle-conditioning, he tells them they are better off learning for themselves. "I'm not trying to be rude, but it is different for everybody," he said.

Here's a short course on how to do it.

Get your sugar right: Michael Hall wrote an excellent primer on bottle-conditioning for homebrewers that first appeared in *Zymurgy* magazine. He points out two vital numbers to know when deciding how much sugar to add for carbonation. The first is the amount of dissolved CO_2 before bottling. For instance, *Duvel* starts bottle-conditioning at 4 to 5 grams per liter (2 to 2.5 volumes). The second is your target CO_2. *Duvel* finishes with 8.5 grams per liter (4.25 volumes) in the bottle. If you are uncertain about calculating how much sugar to use, that article is a fine place to start.[1]

---

[1] Hall, "Brew By the Numbers—Add Up What's in Your Beer," *Zymurgy* 18, no. 2 (Summer 1995): 54-61.

Suppliers in Belgium specialize in priming sugars, but most breweries simply use invert sugar, glucose, or plain sucrose. Any of those will work for an American homebrewer, as will corn sugar. Trappist and abbey beers are bottled at higher carbonation than perhaps any other beer you've packaged, and also at higher rates than have been suggested in the past. Here are a few examples of what levels of carbonation breweries aim for:

- Orval–10 grams per liter/5 volumes.

- Rochefort–7 grams per liter/3.5 volumes.

- Westmalle–6 to 8 grams per liter/3 to 4 volumes.

- Duvel–8.5 grams per liter/4.25 volumes.

- Leffe–6.3 grams per liter/3.1 volumes.

Do you need to re-yeast? Must you go beyond the standard homebrew practice of using whatever yeast remains in beer? If you condition at particularly cold temperatures (such as close to freezing) or for a long period (beyond a month), then it is worth considering. As Thiel eloquently described earlier, conditioning takes place in a harsh environment. The yeast left in your beer has already been through a war. It isn't necessary to use the same yeast as in primary. Trappists do that because they always have it ready. Generally, an alcohol-tolerant strain will do better but is not required. If you don't have a warm room that is truly warm, consider a yeast that performs better at lower temperatures.

Counting yeast: To take an accurate count, you really need a microscope, something in the $250 range. However, you only have to make the correct calculation once, because an estimate will work better with yeast than sugar. After all, the monks at Westvleteren pitch a certain number of buckets of yeast into the bottling tank, and that number varies based on what point in the fermentation process that yeast is cropped. You can also make a good guess based upon the numbers yeast manufacturers provide on the various packages they sell, although the yeast won't be as viable as those taken from a healthy fermentation. There is much be said for taking the Westvleteren approach and pairing brewing and bottling.

Chris White of White Labs estimates a good slurry will contain about 30 to 40% yeast by volume and should have about 1 billion cells per milliliter. You can calculate how much yeast you need from that. Dave Logsdon cautions to be careful in harvesting yeast, particularly from the bottom of the fermenter, because excess trub will wreck your refermentation. "You hate to see a great beer ruined by bad bottle-conditioning, with tons of protein flakes floating in it," he said.

Here are a few examples of the quantities of yeast commercial breweries use in refermentation.

• Duvel–1 million cells per milliliter.

• Orval–3 million cells per milliliter.

• Rochefort–1-plus million cells per milliliter.

• Westmalle–2 million cells per milliliter.

• Allagash–.75 million to 2 million cells per milliliter, depending on the gravity of the beer.

Will your bottles explode? They might. Higher carbonation makes for a better presentation and a beer that is easier to drink, but you must make correct sugar calculations, so you don't end up with a warm room full of bombs. Bottles from many craft beers, which homebrewers recycle, could blow up with 3 volumes of CO_2 in the bottle. There are alternatives. One is to save 330ml bottles from Belgium. A second is to use Champagne-style bottles that accept a crown cap, a solid bet if you have a highly carbonated beer. You might also consider the 750ml bottles that you buy Belgian beers in. However, if you want to seal them with the same mushroom cork as the original, then you'll need a corker, which can get expensive. Plastic champagne corks may work just as well, but these can be tricky. Producers of 750ml bottles make bottles with openings that vary a bit in size, and some can be too large to get a good seal. I have had good success using recycled Ommegang bottles. Simply force the plastic cork in by hand, and clamp it down with a wire enclosure. As soon as your beer begins to referment, the bottle will seal tight.

Be careful when you remove the wire enclosure. The cork may come flying out. When that happens, you know you've done something right.

Brewing Your Own

ten

Matters of Style

*I*n one of the many stories he likes to tell about German, English, and Belgian brewers, Michael Jackson first asks a German how beer is made. "Pils malt, Czech hops," the brewer replies. Then Jackson asks the German brewer down the road the same question. "It's the same as Fritz said. That's how you make a Pilsener, that's what we learn in school."

After getting a different answer from a British brewer, Jackson turns to a Belgian brewer. "First of all, you take one ton of bat's droppings. Then you add a black witch," the Belgian answers. "The brewer down the road uses a white witch." Jackson concludes with the lesson: "Belgium is a nation of tremendous individualists."

If style guidelines for *Bat Dropping Ale* stated that color shouldn't be less than 25 SRM, do you think that would have stopped the brewer down the road from using a white witch? Of course not. Style guidelines don't limit creativity, lack of imagination does.

Speaking of styles, if only in the broadest terms, serves many purposes:

- We add historical perspective and gain insights about how to brew these beers well.

- Styles communicate something about the beer to consumers.

- In competitions, style guidelines provide common ground for brewers and judges, and reduce category entrants to manageable numbers.

- If we didn't make "rules," we wouldn't know when to break them.

The next chapter provides brewing tips for Trappist-inspired beers in broad, "non-stylistic" terms but also leans heavily on the "s" word. That is the context in which brewers created the recipes presented. We lay the ground rules in this chapter, take a different look at the concept of a Trappist family of beers, consider the *inspired* element of Trappist-*inspired*, and acknowledge the value of style guidelines and importance of good judging.

Homebrewer Gordon Strong approaches the subject of Trappist beers and their kin with particular passion. He put together two solid presentations for homebrewers, "Designing Great Dubbels" and "Designing Great Belgian Dark Strong Ales," that helped me get started on this project. He had a major hand in writing the BJCP guidelines and descriptions for these styles, and he contributed to this chapter.

As an engineer, he likes specific information. "Don't tell me to go out and be creative because that's what the Belgians do," he said, when we talked about what he would like to read in this book. "If a Belgian brewer says he doesn't brew to style, it doesn't mean there aren't styles. The Belgian beer came first, and people are trying to categorize it. We aren't trying to dictate to them how to brew."

Some categories emerge in full focus—dubbel and tripel mean something specific to Belgian beer drinkers—but others don't. Carl Kins, a Belgian beer enthusiast who traveled to the United States in 2004 to judge at the 2004 Great American Beer Festival, explains, "We Belgians do not like categorization that much. Whether it is strong blonde ale or abbey style is not very relevant, as long as the beer tastes good."

Nonetheless, the guidelines allowed him to judge Belgian-inspired beers. "To be blunt, as there is such a variety of beer, what I look for in judging is whether the beers fit into the description that is worked out by the Brewers Association," he said.

Phil Markowski tackled the matter of Belgian brewers and style quite well in *Farmhouse Ales*. He writes that brewers of the area often consider themselves artists, which recalls an old adage that farmers make wine and engineers make beer. When it came to brewing, monks were both. Cistercians were afforded a measure of the drink of their region, and in Belgium that didn't mean wine but beer (and buttermilk before the monks began brewing), made for the most part with ingredients they harvested on the grounds. After they decided to sell their beer commercially, most consulted with or hired brewing engineers schooled in the most modern techniques.

That didn't mean they abandoned the nonscientific aspect of brewing. Speaking with Jackson back in the 1980s, Roger Schoonjans, then brewing director at Orval, said: "People should not want our beer to taste exactly the same every time. They want the *Govt d'Orval*, for sure, but they want to be able to chat about it: 'I think this one is a little more hoppy ... yesterday's was rounder ... .' In that respect, they treat it like wine."[1]

TRAPPIST *TERROIR*

To continue on the wine track for a moment more, it seems appropriate that we recognize Trappist as an appellation rather than a style. The *Appellation d'Origine Contrôlée* (AOC) that we associate first with wine is usually region dependent. As small as Belgium is, Trappist ales are brewed in quite different regions. Joris Pattyn, a founding member of Belgium's leading beer consumer group, maintains regionalism influenced the development of these beers at least as much as the more coincidental fact that they are made inside monastery walls.

He does allow for family relations. "I don't want to be extreme; Trappists have influenced each other," Pattyn said.

Chimay may have used a Westvleteren recipe early on, Rochefort took its first one from Achel, and today three monastery breweries share the same yeast. Some interaction was long ago, some continues today, such as the fact that monks from Westmalle and Rochefort provided the modern-day recipes for Achel.

Pattyn makes the point that rather than comparing Trappist-brewed beers only to each other, they should be seen as products of a region. Historically, that makes sense. *Bock* originated in Einbeck, Germany, but developed into the style we know today in Munich for specific regional reasons.

Pattyn has given this some thought. A founding member of *De Objectieve Bierproevers* (a beer consumer group that is now

[1]Jackson, *Great Beers of Belgium* (Philadelphia: Running Press, 1998), 207.

Zythos) in 1985, he has judged at GABF and was one of the authors of *LambicLand* (University Press, 2004), a primer on lambic and guide to lambic cafes in the Payottenland region. He explained in a series of e-mails:

"Westvleteren makes typical West Flemish products. We stare too much at the Saint Bernardus deal. Van Eecke in (nearby) Watou makes similar beers. So did Saint Henricus-Costenoble, the brewery that was to become De Dolle Brouwers. The *Westvleteren Blond* is an allowance to contemporary tastes and preferences. Twenty years ago the range of Westvleteren was sweet-sour, colored beers in a full range of alcohol strength.

"Rochefort and Chimay make a type of beer that is typical for the more eastern regions of Wallonia. Some beers, nowadays less popular, and often known as 'Scotch ale,' are pretty similar to the lesser-alcohol version of the Trappists, such as *Chimay Red* or *Rochefort 6*. The stronger *Chimay Blue* or *Rochefort 8* and *10* have an equivalent in the original *Cuvée de l'Ermitage* (before it was diminished).

"Westmalle has become world famous with their double/triple duo. Originally, they just made a range: 5%, 7%, and 9% abv. Why did Westmalle brew its top beer as a blonde? Because Westmalle is in the province of Antwerp, where strong blonde beers took an earlier foothold than elsewhere. We think of *Duvel*, of *Kastaar*, and others."

Westmalle, Duvel Moortgat, and De Koninck in Antwerp, which makes Belgium's benchmark pale ale, all brew with water softer than in most Belgian breweries, making production of paler beers easier. Nonetheless, *Westmalle Tripel* preceded the paler version of *Duvel* by forty years.

Pattyn continues:

"And then the most interesting, *Orval*. Read all the history about the German brewmaster who perfected the initial recipe with his tartar-covered coppers, which Professor De Clerck had to search back to re-create the 'unique' *Orval* taste. Read today's reports about its triple, mixed fermentation. We are speaking of an original, stronger version of saison. Today's saisons are strong, spicy, and rather sweet, but historically, that was not true. Saison was of mixed fermentation. So is *Orval*, but because of the abbey's demands, this was made stronger already in those days."

Pattyn also offers a story about the danger of confusing styles and designations. More than fifteen years ago, a regional magazine did a comparative test of abbey-style beers. With one notable exception, the panel included wine tasters and journalists, in most cases uninformed about beer. Pattyn explained: "They had a 'dubbel-tripel-whattodowithRochefort' division, and judged accordingly. Among the beers tried was *Felistin*, a truly great little beer—because it was an excellent example of Flemish *Oud Bruin*, relatively low alcohol, sweet-sour. But the eminent tasters in all their ignorance searched it for *Westmalle Dubbel*-like characteristics (it was brown, after all), which of course, it lacked totally. It ended at an abysmal low rating, last of an enormous series. Less than half a year later, *Felistin* was no longer brewed, as no beer seller took it in anymore, all their customers having read the damning words."

He would be happy to see the Brewers Association reunify some of its Belgian styles. "Get rid of the 'abbey' mark," he suggested. "We have strong blonde ales, we have dark sweet-sour beers, we have saisons, we have strong brown roasted beers and light brown ales. Some of them are of the abbey persuasion, some of them are Trappists. But, before the twenty-five years of uniformization struck, they were regionally linked."

BEFORE YOU BREW: CONSULTING VICTOR HORTA

Belgian born and raised, Peter Bouckaert of New Belgium Brewing said that before he was born, his parents hoped their child would grow up to be a priest or a nun. Their second choice was brewer. When Jeff Lebesch and Kim Jordan hired Bouckaert in 1996 to direct brewing at New Belgium, they probably didn't realize the implications. "Not really," Lebesch said. "We didn't understand the depth of his creativity, his insistence in staying away from the average guidelines."

Speaking to an audience of craftbrewers and homebrewers in January 2005, Bouckaert explained how the recipe for *New Belgium 1554*, a black beer, was created. After providing the background, he got to the punchline. "Forget about recipes, forget about kilograms and pounds," he said, raising his voice forcefully. "Forget about style descriptors."

He showed a slide picturing a staircase designed by Belgian architect Victor Horta. "This is inspiring," he said. "When you think of Belgian beer, that's what we are trying to do, trying to create a piece of beauty. Forget about the ingredients I use." He concluded with another slide that showed a pile of words that looked as if they'd been splattered on a page. In larger type amid them were three words: Knowledge, Experience, and Creativity. "Those are the three things you need. I don't use yeast and malt, I only use this."

A View From the Continent

Derek Walsh was born in Toronto, Canada, and started homebrewing after moving to Holland in 1985. After winning the national homebrew competition in 1985 and 1986, he decided to follow national beer judge training and became certified in 1987. He co-founded the SNAB brewing foundation and developed 11 commercial beers from 1991 to 2001. He published *"Biertypen Gids"* (a guide to beer styles) and began his part-time consultancy B.I.E.R.+ in 2002. He currently lectures and judges on invitation (one of the more recent competitions was the 2004 World Beer Cup).

Have you seen Trappist beers change in the last ten years, and how?

Yes. Dubbels: Lower original gravities, higher attenuation, and lower IBUs. Tripels: Relatively stable. Quadrupels (known as dark strong ale by American homebrewers): Lower original gravities, higher attenuations, and lower IBUs. The worst hit in my opinion is *Chimay Blue*, which may be partially due to changing their fermentation tanks.

How about abbey beers, and how?

Yes. Lower original gravities, higher attenuations, and lower IBUs, and increased use of sugars, extracts, and "God knows what else."

Are abbey beers more or less like Trappist beers than in the past?

Less. This is giving the Trappists the edge they need to survive.

Do Belgian consumers perceive a difference between Trappist and abbey beers?

Not really. Most Belgian pubs call abbey beers Trappists, and without the beer consumer confederation *Zythos* and its twenty-two local associations doing their utmost to inform and educate, the general public wouldn't have a clue or care. On the positive side, the perception that Trappist beers are better in quality is definitely growing.

In judging at the World Beer Cup, what misconceptions about Belgian styles did you see?

The only Belgian style categories that I judged were Saison and Belgian- and French-Style

A View From the Continent, continued

Ale, so I can't give inside opinions about other categories; however, I did see (and taste) the results of other categories, and I feel that there is too much emphasis on "funkiness" (medicinal off-flavors, overpowering use of spices, specialty malts, and sugars).

Why define styles?

You've got to start somewhere! All beginning cooks and artists look back at what their successful predecessors did and learn to understand the basic techniques and materials used. This background gives them the freedom to be able to let their creative juices flow and produce something truly inspirational.

What is different about the way Continental homebrewers approach these styles?

They have access to fresh, non-light-struck, non-container-boiled/vibrated or otherwise damaged examples. They can often meet the brewers or their representatives to gain more insight into the process and ingredients, and they can get access to those ingredients.

Do you think there is such a thing as a dark tripel? If no, was there ever?

No. Once a tripel's color gets up to around 20 EBC (8 SRM), it becomes cloying and loses its refreshing qualities. The Anker brewery in Mechelen, Belgium, made a 7.3% abv "dark tripel" called *Toison d'Or* from 1983 to approximately 2001 that was around 30 to 35 EBC (15 to 17 SRM). They replaced this beer with their blonder and stronger 9% abv *Gouden Carolus Tripel* in 2002. It won a gold in the World Beer Cup tripel category in 2002.

Careful research reveals that New Belgium does, in fact, brew with yeast and malt. Bouckaert directs one of the most modern breweries in the world, overseeing 2,500 brews a year. When he talks about the need for a brewer to adapt and experiment, in his case that means bringing larger fermenters on line, making sure that *Blue Paddle Pilsener* tastes the same when fermented in a 720-hectoliter (613-barrel) tank as it did in a 360-hectoliter tank. He demands technical excellence, then asks for more.

"Maybe the craftbrewers were (once) looking to the Old World, Germany, Great Britain, then Belgium. Is it really about the Old World?" he asked. "Let's create something, let's have fun."

Jean-Marie Rock, brewing director at Orval since the early 1990s, puts a different twist on that thought. "Before copying Belgian brewers or Belgian methods, tell the American brewers that they have to produce a specific beer made for the American people," he said.

But is this about copying methods or learning from them?

"I try to re-create some of the beers I enjoyed there," said Markowski, who has visited Belgium often. "But also, more important to me, I try to do something within the Belgian spirit, which is brewing something unique."

Ron Jeffries of Jolly Pumpkin Ales, who wrote the blonde ale recipe for this book although he has never brewed one, talks about it as a journey. "In brewing great beer, especially Belgian-style beer, don't become hung up on the guidelines, on the numbers. Think about the flavors," he said. "I brew to the taste. To the vision. Not to the guidelines. This was not always so for me. For years I followed the guidelines, trying to perfectly match any given style. Like the aspiring artist practicing year after year, painting a solitary stick of bamboo, exactingly replicating the master's work. Only after years of painstaking perfection is the student allowed to add a leaf here, a sprig there. Such can be brewing. After years of pale ale, English versus American, porter, stout, robust, brown, and the like, I began to brew differently. Asking not just how it should taste, but how I want it to taste."

Brit Antrim of Kona Brewing Company in Hawaii was at Anderson Valley Brewing Company when the California brewery created *Brother David's*, a dubbel, for David Keene at San Francisco's Toronado pub. The beer started out tasting much like Anderson Valley's *Boont Amber Ale*. "I grew a little more willing to throw caution to the wind and try something new," Antrim said. His thoughts after judging Belgian styles at the 2004 Great American Beer Festival: "Strive to make your own unique beer. Too many try to duplicate a known beer. If I wanted a *Chimay Grande Réserve*, I would buy one. Try to set your own mark."

Back in Chapter 6 we visited American brewers who understand the idea. They have taken ales that might once have been brewed in a monastery and expanded on them, creating beers such as *Curieux*, Allagash Brewing's barrel-aged tripel. These brewers represent a larger group. For instance:

- In 2004 Will Meyers at Cambridge Brewing Company in Massachusetts, a brewpub that began serving Belgian-style beers well before many Americans brewed them, conjured up a beer called *Benevolence*. He brewed it with candi sugar (rocks); fermented it with three yeasts, one English and two Belgian; conditioned it in Jack Daniel's barrels with honey, sour cherries, date sugar, and a lambic strain; then aged it in the barrel for 18 months before blending it with a 12% abv barley wine. *Benevolence* won a medal at the Great American Beer Festival.

- When Dogfish Head Brewery rolled out *Raison D'Etre* in the late 1990s, the brewery played on a Belgian connection, noting the use of Belgian beet sugar, raisins, and a Belgian yeast, but never advertising the beer as a "Belgian style." "We made our own interpretation of an off-centered ale while still acknowledging the Belgian trend," said founder Sam Calagione.

• In 2002 Stone Brewing Company in California began a series of Vertical Epic Ales, single batches released once a year, beginning on February 2, 2002, then on March 3, 2003, etc., with plans to roll out the last on December 12, 2012. Stone brewed each of the first four with a Belgian yeast strain, but when the fourth was released, CEO Greg Koch said: "Our Stone Vertical Epic Ales are 'Belgian' in the same way that our *Stone Ruination IPA* is 'British.' ... Yes, the *Stone 05.05.05 Vertical Epic Ale* is brown. Yes, we used a Belgian yeast strain. However, it is unquestionably as much or more a Stone beer (i.e., nontraditional) as it is a Belgian-styled beer."

Several California brewers began a discussion in 2002 that was ongoing in 2005, suggesting it is time to designate a family of American Abbey beers. Tomme Arthur of the Pizza Port brewery and Tom Nickel, another brewer, made their argument in a hobby publication: "(American Abbey beers are) creative, artistic beers purposely brewed not to any current category designation. These unique beers were not Belgian-style and went where no Belgian beer had."[2]

Trappist brewers once went where no other Belgian brewers had, and capture our imagination because they are rooted in both tradition and innovation. Early in 2005 Yvan De Baets, the enthusiast-historian who wrote the history of saison in

[2] Arthur and Nickel, "Don't Call It a Belgian . . . ," *Zymurgy* 28: 2 (March-April 2005): 33.

Farmhouse Ales, talked about tradition while sampling beers he had carefully cellared since the early 1990s. We followed three vintages of *Orval* with a bottle of Russian River Brewing's *Temptation,* which, like *Orval,* is infused with *Brettanomyces,* but then is aged in Chardonnay barrels.

De Baets smiled in approval. "That guy (Russian River brewer Vinnie Cilurzo) is headed in the right direction," he said. "He chose good *Brett,* not everybody does that. These kinds of wild yeast are one thing that makes Belgian brewers different. Now it comes back like a boomerang."

This book doesn't deal with wild yeast strains, except in the context that they influence *Orval* and *Temptation.* It's about traditional beers brewed in the most traditional of surroundings in a very modern world. De Baets stepped forward in 1993 when he thought *Orval* had lowered the bar, and he still doesn't offer any brewery a free pass based on tradition. Instead, he provides important perspective on Trappists, Belgian brewing, and even American craftbrewing when he talks about a boomerang.

"One of the main goals of Belgian brewers should be to fight against the Coca-Cola flavors and those kind of gadget tastes," he said. "We should be about cultural tastes, not animal tastes."

JUDGING: GETTING IT RIGHT

Just as brewers need to understand what these styles born in Belgium taste like, so do judges. In theory, better judging is an ingredient in better brewing. I asked Gordon Strong to detail how he thinks judges can do better. His comments were written in the context of judging homebrewed beers, but also relate to evaluating or simply enjoying commercial products.

I've participated in more than one hundred competitions, and have probably judged more than 3,000 beers and entered several hundred. As Belgian beers are among my favorite styles, I've had my share of experiences both as a brewer and a judge. I've witnessed many judging errors.

The biggest judging error is not understanding the full range of Belgian beer styles. Many styles (such as Belgian Dark Strong Ale) are quite broad and cannot be accurately defined by a single commercial example. If a judge has a "halo effect" from his favorite example and ignores the style guidelines, he is doing a disservice to the brewer. Belgians prize artisanal creativity, so don't dismiss a beer because it isn't a clone of your favorite brew.

Many judges also exhibit "big beer bias." Inexperienced judges often show a marked preference for higher alcohol or more intensely flavored beers. Just as choosing the strongest barley wine and the most bitter IPA isn't necessarily the right choice, selecting a Belgian beer on the basis of alcohol content, fusels, or aggressive yeast by-products (especially phenolics) is often misguided. Look to the overall balance of the beer, not simply the intensity of individual components.

Many new judges seem to look for reasons not to evaluate a beer, preferring to disqualify an entry for technical "violations" of the style guidelines. For example, a relatively pale Belgian dark strong can still be quite good, as can a tripel with mild spicing. Focusing on a perceived negative and drawing unnecessary conclusions almost always short-changes the brewer. I've seen many judges ding a wonderful dark strong ale because it's not dark brown. It's hard to get malt flavor complexity in a beer that's very pale, so lighter-colored dark strongs may deserve to get dinged for that reason. Unfortunately, I think the color prejudices many judges as to what flavors they therefore expect.

The 2004 style guidelines also tend to correct past misunderstandings about specific flavors. For instance, the 1999 guidelines discussed phenolics as being acceptable in many styles but didn't offer any detail. Many judges would automatically assume this means "clovelike," as in a hefeweizen. However, in most Belgian beers, the phenolic overtone most desirable is one reminiscent of black pepper. Likewise, smoky, medicinal, or plasticlike phenolics are undesirable. "Estery" doesn't mean "bananalike" in most Belgians, either. Understanding the correct type of ester, phenol, alcohol, malt, and hops for a given beer style is an important milestone in the training of a beer judge.

A related phenomenon is not deducting for (or even detecting) faults in a beer. Perhaps this is due to an incomplete understanding of beer styles, or a desire for aggressive beers, but many high-scoring Belgian beers often have significant faults. For example, many Belgian dark strongs have excessive fusel alcohols. Some may enjoy this, but most experienced judges would rather avoid the "headache flight." I recall one competition where a judge accurately described the fusels in a beer "like a flaming hot railroad spike driven into your temple." Yet, other judges at the table wanted this beer to be awarded first place.

Judges should be able to understand the beer style being judged, recognize a proper balance, nuance, and artisanal effort by a brewer, and to point out flaws such as excessive body, sweetness, lack of attenuation, undercarbonation, burning alcohol finish, and out-of-balance flavors. It does no good to give poor feedback to a brewer (either by rewarding an inferior effort or not recognizing a wonderful beer), since that tends to encourage the wrong behavior. Beer judges should provide structured analysis and feedback to brewers to help them understand how their brews stack up against world-class examples and to give advice in how to improve their results. Anything less is just an exercise in handing out ribbons without meaning.

—*Gordon Strong*

eleven

Recipes: What Works

ore than fifty years ago, the monks of Rochefort faced something of a crisis, because consumers in their backyard quite obviously preferred "new and improved" beers from Chimay. Chimay wasn't about to quit selling beer in Rochefort's neighborhood, but offered technical support, recipes, and apparently even its yeast. Ultimately, Rochefort decided what worked for Chimay didn't work at Rochefort. The brewery used its own recipes and different yeast, and to this day brews beers of the same high quality as Chimay.

That makes sense to Ron Ryan of malt supplier Cargill, once a brewer himself. "There are very few real secrets in brewing," he said. "You could have every recipe from every brewery, every detail, their mashing, their fermentation temperatures, and you wouldn't have their beer."

In this chapter, a variety of brewers offer specific details about recipes and brewing, but like Rochefort in the 1950s, you'll do best if you think of them in the context of your own brewery.

First we'll examine fundamental keys for brewing any of these styles well, before considering them individually. For the sake of convenience, I've organized the chapter along Beer Judge Certification Program guidelines (*www.bjcp.org*) to organize categories. For similar Brewers Association guidelines, visit *www.beertown.org*. Each category starts with an overview, then includes guidelines, a look at what a few commercial examples look like, and data on how award-winning homebrewers interpret the styles. For each style, a professional or amateur brewer created a recipe.

About the Recipe Data

Four of the categories listed include information about how homebrewers approach making these beers. I acquired the data in an entirely unscientific way. Homebrewers submitted recipes to a website that I created to supplement research. Those recipes with some sort of pedigree—that is, they won a medal in a decent-sized competition—are represented with these tables. Each of the categories shown includes information from about thirty recipes, except for blonde ales, because only a handful of blonde ale recipes were submitted. Do I think the recipes represent the entire universe of homebrew efforts? No. I do think they represent beers that do well in competitions. I'll leave it to you to decide the importance of that.

The tables should be self-explanatory. In the case of the tables for "characteristics," rather than listing final gravity, apparent attenuation is included, because final gravity means more if you know starting gravity. In the tables that show grain bills, "incidence" indicates in what percentage of the recipes the ingredients were used. With the relatively low number of recipes, some ingredients may be over-represented. For instance,

What Doesn't Work

Victory Brewing Company in Pennsylvania earned a reputation for being able to brew just about any style well. Hopheads love the flagship *HopDevil Ale*, the tripel-ish *Golden Monkey* became the brewery's second-best seller, and *Men's Journal* called *Prima Pils*, a delightfully German Pilsener, the best craft beer in the United States and the best Pilsener in the world.

And then there was *V-Ten*. "Part of the V-series idea was to challenge ourselves, make beers that we were not necessarily totally on top of. That went awry with the *V-Ten*, but it's an interactive process," said co-founder Bill Covaleski. Partner Ron Barchet talked candidly about what went wrong. "It had a lot of dark malt, a lot of dark candi sugar. There was something about our wort, it just didn't attenuate," he said. As a result, some customers opened bottles of beer that they loved, while others poured an infected product. The *V-Ten* kicked off a Belgian series, and *V-Twelve* and

Grand Cru fared much better. Barchet didn't give up on the *V-Ten* without a fight.

"We tried everything in our second year," Barchet said. "We grew up the yeast more, but we just couldn't get the right attenuation. It was under 60%. There was just too much for bugs to get in." Victory pulled the plug on *V-Ten*. Barchet continues to work on the *Grand Cru* and *V-Twelve*, the latter an intriguing beer that even when young starts to show portlike qualities. It starts big at 1.115 (27 °P), with two 50-barrel batches fermented using different yeasts that are blended into one beer. On the latest batch, one yeast attenuated very well, and the other came up quite short. "We are always going to make this with two strains," Barchet said, although he was shopping for a replacement for the second. "We've only made three 100-barrel batches. Those (attenuation) numbers are not going to be the same in two years."

I doubt 7% of all homebrewed tripels use honey. "Average" means the average percentage of the ingredient used across all the recipes (which is why honey registers at less than .5 %).

Brewing With Extracts

The recipes presented here include all-grain (and sugar) malt bills. Can you brew these beers with extract? Yes, although as homebrewer Gordon Strong points out, he was motivated to begin all-grain brewing so he could mash for fermentability when brewing a dubbel. "The problem I have with most malt extracts (dry or liquid) is that I don't know what type(s) of grain was used in its preparation," he said. "Most Belgian beers feature a rich malt profile; for example, a tripel has a flavorful Pilsener malt flavor and a dubbel or dark strong ale often has a rich, complex Munich and/or Vienna malt flavor. Most malt extracts are made with U.S. or U.K. grain; even premium extracts might use something inappropriate like Maris Otter. Worse, many might use U.S. six-row or other inferior-tasting grain. The problem gets worse with darker extracts. Where did the color come from? What flavors are also present? A dark extract with roasted barley would be fine for a stout but all wrong for a dark strong ale."

Some of the rules are the same as with any extract beer. "Make sure you have fresh extract (stale extract often has a 'tangy' flavor), use the lightest-colored extract you can find, do a 'mini-mash' to add additional flavor and body, pitch plenty of healthy, active yeast, aerate (or oxygenate), and make sure sufficient nutrients are available (I like the Wyeast nutrient mix)," Strong said.

Dave Logsdon of Wyeast said is impossible to overestimate the importance of fresh extract. "One of the things we see with extract is that most of it is somewhat oxidized," he said. "It gives you an estery profile that can be cidery. It ruins the potential for something that shows off the yeast's aromatics in a positive way. When you start with good-quality extract, you'll be surprised by the character that comes through."

My suggestion would be to conduct a mini-mash (if you can steep, you can manage a mash with 60% efficiency) for as much of the base as you can, probably with American malts. Because they are higher in soluble protein, they permit you to use more sugar. The higher percentage of extract you include, the less sugar you should use.

WHAT WE'VE LEARNED

Most of what works when brewing a Trappist-inspired blonde-colored strong ale works just as well when brewing a dark strong ale. Keys to successfully brewing beers in this family include:

- Use quality Pilsener malt, or more than one, for the base. Paler styles may include only Pilsener and sugar, although 1 to 3% of Munich or a light-colored caramel malt will add complexity.

- If you're using malt extract, find a reliably fresh pale extract and get all your color from specialty grains. That way, you have control over the recipe.

- Balance specialty malts and dark sugar for complexity in darker beers. Limit malts darker than 40 °L to 7% of the grist.

- Modify your brewing water as you usually do, making adjustments for pH, particularly in lighter-colored beers.

Consult the water tables (p. 158) to emulate water for a particular brewing region. Consider adding calcium carbonate (chalk) to boost bicarbonate levels into the range of 200-250 parts per million when brewing darker beers.

- Mash for attenuation. Use a single-infusion mash between 146 and 149° F (63 to 65° C) or consider a step mash such as at Ommegang. However, remember there is a chance with highly modified malts that a step mash (the protein rest, specifically) may degrade proteins too much and can cause a loss of body and head. With beers that have some sugar in them, the danger is greater.

- Use sugar for 10 to 20% of grist.

- Use the right sugar. Sucrose works to add gravity and lighten the body. Caramelized sugar adds necessary flavors to dark beers, including an elusive rumminess, that dark candi sugar (rocks) won't. Some American craftbrewers use turbinado or other semi-refined sugars to add lovely rummy overtones. American brown sugar won't work as a substitute.

- Use "noble-type" hops, with bittering hops accounting for two-thirds of the hop mass and the flavor addition at thirty minutes remaining in the boil. Aim for a BU:GU ratio of about 3:8, a little higher for tripels and lower for strong darks.

- Spice with care. Spices may add complexity but cannot substitute for fermentation character. If a drinker can name the spice, you've used too much.

- Pitch enough viable yeast, using a starter or yeast from a previous fermentation (top cropped if possible). Consider experimenting with a lower pitching rate, but remember, it's an experiment.

- Pick a yeast with the flavor characteristics you want, perhaps experimenting with split batches. Then stick to that yeast, experimenting with how it reacts across a range of conditions.

- Consider blending yeast strains to add complexity.

- Don't be afraid of higher fermentation temperatures, but consider pitching lower than the low end of the recommended temperature range and allowing the temperature to rise throughout fermentation.

- Let the fermentation finish, perhaps at a higher temperature. It may take as long to get the last few points of attenuation as it did for the first 80%.

- Allow for longer-than-average secondary fermentation and further long cold conditioning before bottling.

- Bottle-condition, re-yeast when bottle-conditioning, and condition to high levels of CO_2 in a warm room. Let the beer continue to condition at a cooler temperature after it has carbonated.

- Resign yourself to the fact that the recipe perfect for your taste might not be a recipe that does well in competition.

Pros: Tips From Judges

First of all, brewing Belgian beer isn't black magic; basic brewing skills still matter. "The mistakes I see usually are not just restricted to Belgian styles," said John Kimmich of the Alchemist Pub & Brewery in Vermont. "If a brewer makes beers that are solid across the bar, their Belgians usually are as well."

Research ought to be fun. "My best resource has been drinking Belgian beers, both here in the States and in Belgium," said George de Piro of C.H. Evans Brewing Company in Albany, New York. "The condition of the beer makes a huge difference in its flavor profile. It is important to recognize the difference between the flavors of aged beer and fresh when trying to emulate a specific beer, which is why it is so important to go to Belgium for fresh examples."

Casey Gwinn of Three Rivers Eatery and Brewhouse in New Mexico added: "Many Belgian beers have more subtle flavors than their American counterparts. A bigger hammer isn't always better. I see a ton of high-gravity, big-assed Belgian beers, and only a few of their more subtle-gravity brethren."

Those who have judged at GABF offer nuggets:

- Understand the style, most notably phenolics and mouthfeel.
- Understand the categories, and enter the correct one.
- Avoid underattenuation, beer that is too sweet.
- Avoid hot higher alcohol, fusels. Pitch a proper amount of yeast, and assure proper aeration.
- Avoid distinctive American hops, and don't make the beer too hoppy.
- Don't try to use spices to substitute for dryness that can be achieved through attenuation.
- Be careful of dimethyl sulfide in tripels and strong goldens. Don't forgo a vigorous boil to avoid color increase.
- Use sugar. An all-malt beer likely will end up too sweet and cloying.
- Carbonate to appropriate levels.

Vinnie Cilurzo of Russian River Brewing points to a more subtle challenge—not aging the beer long enough before it is served or shipped out. "Belgian-style ales or anything closely resembling them cannot be treated the same as an IPA, porter, etc.," he said. "They require more aging to round out their subtle flavors. Unfortunately, in a brewpub setting the brewer is pushed to get the product out on a 21-day or shorter cycle. I like to point out the long voyage the beers have in a container on the water as they are shipped over here to the United States. They probably are sitting on the water for at least two months before they get here. Bottom line, American brewers just don't or can't age the Belgian styles long enough to develop their unique character."

BLONDE ALE

When Westvleteren introduced *Westvleteren Blond* (and discontinued two darker beers) in 1999 to celebrate renovating its café opposite the abbey, even the least commercial of the monastery brewers was acknowledging the popularity of paler beers. Although the monks produced something the color of the certified abbey beers that define this style, they brewed a beer that otherwise was very different.

Commercial breweries making abbey beer created blonde ales to compete with popular Pilseners without being as alcoholic as tripels or golden strongs. BJCP guidelines accurately describe the blondes (known as blond by the BJCP): "Similar strength as a dubbel, similar character as a Belgian Strong Golden Ale or tripel, although a bit sweeter and not as bitter." *Leffe Blond* and *Grimbergen Blond*, for instance, aim for the broadest possible audience and finish sweet.

Table 11.1 Blonde Style Guidelines, Commercial Examples

	Original Gravity SG (°Plato)	Alcohol (abv)	Apparent Extract FG (°Plato)	Color SRM (EBC)	Bitterness IBU
BJCP	1.062-1.075 (15.2-18.2 °P)	6-7.5%	1.008-1.016 (2.1-4.1 °P)	4-6 (8-12)	20-30
Leffe Blond	1.06 (15.6 °P)	6.6%	1.013 (3.3 °P)	6.5 (13)	25
Westvleteren Blond	1.051 (12.6 °P)	5.6%	1.008 (2.1 °P)	4.5 (9)	41
La Trappe Blond	1.061 (14.9 °P)	6.7%	1.010 (2.6 °P)	9 (18)	14

Color measured in EBC, converted to SRM by dividing by 1.97 (see p. 18).

The most representative examples feature almost entirely Pilsener malts, although some pale or Munich may be added for subtle complexity; are hopped at a BU:GU rate of 3:8 or less; and count on yeast to deliver a fruity, spicy experience.

Many Belgian breweries label their beer "blond," although it would not fit in the BJCP guidelines (no comparable BA guidelines exist), and they remind us of the freedom we expect when brewing with Belgian inspiration. Westvleteren's starts at a modest 1.051 (12.6 °P) and delivers bitterness (41 IBUs) throughout. Brasserie Caracole's *Saxo*, labeled as a blonde ale, starts at 1.065 (16 °P) and finishes with 8% abv. Although it has been described as *Duvel*-like, François Tonglet of Caracole accurately describes *Saxo* as "triple white beer," and unmalted wheat in the grain bill adds to that impression. "We wanted a quite fresh taste, and a fine but present bitterness. That's why we used Saaz (hops)," he said.

Examples featured in this book: *Leffe Blond, Affligem Blonde, Saxo, Westvleteren Blond, De Koninck Blond*

Amateurs: Learn to Spot Faults

Knowing how to do things right means being able to identify flaws, but that fact seems harder for brewers to understand when it comes to these styles. This paragraph appeared in a homebrewing magazine article that included otherwise useful information to help readers brew better Belgian beers: "Don't look for faults. Most Belgian ales are their own style and don't conform to BJCP guidelines. You will have to look opposite of how most of us judge and evaluate beer."

That's plain wrong. We accentuate the positive in this chapter, including suggestions for how to successfully brew Trappist-inspired styles. But for a moment we'll get critical, passing along faults judges who contributed to this book see too often:

- Too many higher alcohols, too fusel, solvency.
- Too many spices, or too much of a single spice.
- Too hoppy, wrong (American) hops.
- Wrong yeast (particularly, substituting a wheat yeast).

- Infected (don't enter a beer as Belgian when it becomes infected, or try to stick band-aid beers in this category).
- Too sweet (usually underattenuated, or too much malt because of a fear of sugar).
- Lacking complexity (the great challenge—Trappist malt bills are usually simple, with yeast and time filling in the blanks).
- Too fruity, too much banana, too much clove.

Don't be discouraged. Marc Limet at Brouwerij Kerkom was once an amateur brewer. "A lot of homebrewers make it too difficult," he said. "One asked me questions, each step he takes a bottle and measures something. I ask him if the taste is good. If it is, why must you do this? A lot of brewers must learn to brew with water, malt, yeast, and hops—start like the Germans brew beer. If you can do that, then don't worry. If you have troubles with beer, then you start looking."

The recipe

Ron Jeffries of Jolly Pumpkin Artisan Ales created this recipe. He started with preliminary thoughts: "Key in writing a great recipe is to begin with the end. You must begin with the finished beer. You need a very clear vision of the beer you wish to brew. How does it look, what color is it? What shade, what highlights? Does it  glow; does it sparkle, or throw a yeasty haze? How does the head look, its color, texture, and lacing? Breathe in deeply through your nose. How does it smell? What does the aroma tell you about the beer? Mmmm, now taste it. How is it? Good, I hope! Try to pick out the nuances, and any clues they give you of the beer's ingredients, and brewing. Is it malty, hoppy? Balanced? How so? What are the flavors, what are the flavors, what are the flavors? Just as the sculptor looks at a block of stone and sees the final sculpture, so must be the brewer.

"In brewing great beer, especially Belgian-styled beer, don't become hung up on the guidelines, on the numbers. Think about the flavors. Buy some commercial examples, if you like."

He looked at the guidelines, but they "would have to be just that, guidelines. A launching point if you will," he said. "So I imagined my beer: Blonde and glowing and slightly hazy. Clean white head, tiny bubbles, clinging lace. Subtle fruit, pronounced grassy wheat and spicy lemon, gentle hops, yum."

Jeffries suggests some surprises: "Lemongrass, lemon balm, verbena, and maybe a touch (read very small amount) of peel. Amount of each spice to use is a tough one. Generally best to

Ron Jeffries' Blond Ale

Original Gravity: 1.055 (13.6 °P)

Final Gravity: 1.013 (3.3 °P)

Racking Gravity: 1.008

Alcohol by Volume: 6.0%

IBU: 27

Grist Bill:

  Pilsener malt 60%

  Wheat malt (European) 33%

  Dextrose 7% to kettle

Hops:

  First addition, Styrian Goldings, second, Hallertau
  Or maybe Crystal

err on the side of caution. I would use one short stalk of lemon-grass, and roughly four leaves each of lemon balm and lemon verbena, and maybe 1 ounce (or less) of dried peel per barrel (28 grams per 117 liters). Lightly crush the stalks and leaves directly before use. This should give us just the hint of lemon perfume I'm looking for in the aroma, and flavor towards the finish. If you can't find all the plants, don't sweat it, the beer will be great without them. Instead, try using about 1 ounce per barrel (31 gallons) Crystal as a finishing hop at the end of boil to bring in some gentle aroma."

He favors mashing at 147° F (64° C) for fermentability, and running off at a slowish pace. Boil for 90 minutes, with the first hop addition (66% contribution to IBU) at the beginning of the boil, and the remainder at the one-hour mark. Spices are dropped in (use a nylon bag) at the end of boil.

Ferment with White Labs WLP550. Jeffries uses open fermenters, with a circulating pump for aeration. "After that, just stand back and let it happen. Once fermentation kicks in, I rarely cool these yeasts," he said. "If cooled at the wrong time, they have the tendency to stall at an unfortunately high gravity, and take forever to finish, if they do at all. It's not uncommon for me to let the 550 reach temperatures of 84 to 86° F (29 to 30° C) in the summer months. Trust me, it's OK. After reaching 'final' gravity I let the beer cool itself down, taking its time, and in about four or five days you should reach your racking gravity."

Condition for four to five weeks at ambient temperature, and then bottle, re-yeasting at a rate of about one-tenth of the original pitching yeast. Cellar the bottled beer to develop more flavor.

Table 11.2 Strong Pale/Golden Style Guidelines, Commercial Examples

	Original Gravity SG (°Plato)	Alcohol (abv)	Apparent Extract (FG)	Color SRM (EBC)	Bitterness IBU
BJCP	1.070-1.095 (17.1-22.7 °P)	7.5-10%	1.010-1.016 (2.6-4.1 °P)	4-6 (8-12)	25-35
Brewers Association	1.064-1.096 (16-23 °P)	7-11%	1.012-1.024 (3-6 °P)	3.5-7 (7-14)	20-50
Duvel	1.069 (16.9 °P)	8.4%	1.006 (1.5 °P)	3.5 (7)	30
Malheur 10	1.083 (20 °P)	10.1%	1.007 (1.8 °P)	5.5 (11)	33
Avery Salvation	1.080 (19.3 °P)	9%	1.012 (3.1 °P)	n/a	28

Color measured in EBC, converted to SRM by dividing by 1.97 (see p. 18).

Table 11.3 Characteristics for
Homebrewed Golden Strong Ales

	Low	High	Average
SG	1.065 (15.9 °P)	1.088 (21.1 °P)	1.080
abv	6.7%	9.6%	8.7%
Apparent Attenuation	73%	92%	82%
IBU	26	44	35
BU:GU	0.29	0.65	0.43
SRM	4	12	7

Table 11.4 Grain Bills for
Homebrewed Golden Strong Ales

	Low	High	Average	Incidence
Pilsener	10%	92%	85%	100%
Pale	0	80%	0.5%	11%
Munich/aromatic	0	5%	1%	30%
Cara, crystal	0	8%	1%	30%
Wheat	0	12%	0.5%	14%
Sugar	6%	18%	12%	100%
Spices	-	-	-	4%

GOLDEN AND STRONG

Michael Jackson pretty much named the style when he called
Duvel a strong golden ale in his *New World Guide to Beer*. The
BJCP category calls this golden strong ale, and the BA guidelines
Belgian-style pale strong ale, while continental style author
Derek Walsh prefers strong blonde as a descriptor. We'll use
golden strong ale in the interest of consistency. Although you

might have thought evolution would have worked another way, this style emerged well after tripel and about the same time as golden-colored beers called "blonde."

In providing a recipe for this style, Vinnie Cilurzo of Russian River Brewing Company mentions the similarities between what might be called a golden strong and a tripel. Walsh points to the numbers that set *Westmalle Tripel* and *Duvel* apart, since those are the benchmarks for their respective styles. But look at the specifications for a number of beers, and the differences within the golden strong family are as big as between tripels and golden strongs. For instance, in a tasting of Dutch and Belgian tripels conducted in 2004, *Malheur 10* from Brouwerij De Landtsheer, which was fermented with Westmalle yeast, placed first, ahead of *Westmalle Tripel* and *Chimay White*. However, the brewery entered the beer as a pale strong ale in the 2004 World Beer Cup, where it finished third. I have listed it with the strong goldens here, but its numbers wouldn't look out of place with the tripels.

Lyle Brown, a homebrewer and homebrew judge who has also judged at GABF, agrees about the confusion. "The bottom line is the yeast," he said. "What is the difference between *Chimay White* and *Duvel*? The yeasty spiciness. The golden strong emphasizes fruity strength, the tripel spicy strength."

Duvel uses only Pilsener malts and dextrose sugar in its grist, taking careful measures throughout to keep color as light as possible. The addition of other malts such as pale, CaraPils, or Munich should be kept to a minimum. Better examples have a BU:GU ratio of about 2:5 and finish dry to bone dry. Many breweries in Belgium produce a beer along these lines with a name implying the devil and find some consumers prefer

Vinnie Cilurzo's Strong Golden Ale

Original Gravity: 1.066-1.072 (16.1-17.5 °P)

Final Gravity: 1.006-1.012 (1.5-3.1 °P)

Alcohol by Volume: 7-8%

IBU: 23-33

Grist Bill:

Pilsener malt 80%-100%

Wheat malt 2.5-5% (optional)

Munich malt 2.5-5% (optional)

Sugar (candi rocks, turbinado, or dextrose) 5%-20%

Hops:

Styrian Goldings, 90 minutes, 30% hop bill (13-15 IBU)

Styrian Goldings, 30 minutes, 35% hop bill (7-10 IBU)

Saaz, at knockout, 35% of hop bill (3-5 IBU)

Mash: 151-152° F (66-67° C)

Yeast: White Labs WLP500 or Wyeast 1214

Fermentation: Dependent on yeast choice, 66-76° F (19-24° C)

sweeter versions. One, perhaps trying to more closely emulate *Duvel*, recently boosted its apparent attenuation from 70% to 80% and saw its sales drop dramatically.

Examples featured in this book: *Duvel, Damnation, PranQster, Salvation*

The recipe

Ask Cilurzo to describe the perfect beer, and you'll get something that sounds a lot like *Duvel*. But don't call this a clone of *Duvel* or *Damnation*, because Cilurzo has given you a range to work in. Remember, brewing is about choices.

"Brewing a strong golden ale to me is about having an end product that is dry," he said. "The lines are blurred between a tripel and a strong golden ale, but to me, strong golden ales are drier than most tripels. In many cases a tripel may have more hops, but there seems to be more residual sweetness as well. Also, I like to define strong golden ales as being lighter in color and lighter in the mouth than a tripel.

"We brew *Damnation* to an end abv of 7% straight up. While we were at Korbel, I had *Damnation* as high as 8% abv but found that it was more drinkable and sellable at 7% abv. This also leaves me more room to do a tripel someday. If that day ever comes, we'd have *Damnation* out as our standard year-round brew, and a tripel as a special release, and having more distance between the two, especially in abv, will make both beers more distinctive."

Table 11.5 Tripel Style Guidelines, Commercial Examples

	Original Gravity SG (°Plato)	Alcohol (abv)	Apparent Extract (FG)	Color SRM (EBC)	Bitterness IBU
BJCP	1.075-1.085 (18.2-20.4 °P)	7.5-9%	1.010-1.016 (2.6-4.1 °P)	4.5-6 (9-12)	25-38
Brewers Association	1.060-1.096 (15-24 °P)	7-10%	1.008-1.020 (2-5 °P)	3.5-7 (7-14)	20-25
Westmalle Tripel	1.081 (19.6 °P)	9.6%	1.010 (2.6 °P)	6.5 (13)	39
Affligem Tripel	1.076 (18.4 °P)	8.3%	1.013 (3.3 °P)	6.5 (13)	31
La Rulles Tripel	1.075 (18.2 °P)	8.3%	1.013 (3.3 °P)	9 (18)	23

Color measured in EBC, converted to SRM by dividing by 1.97 (see page 18).

Table 11.6 Characteristics for Homebrewed Tripels

	Low	High	Average
SG	1.072 (17.5 °P)	1.092 (22 °P)	1.084
abv	7.7%	10.6%	9%
Apparent Attenuation	68%	88%	82%
IBU	22	44	32
BU:GU	0.27	0.52	0.38
SRM	5	10	7

Table 11.7 Grain Bills for Homebrewed Tripels

	Low	High	Average	Incidence
Pilsener	75%	90%	83%	100%
Pale	0	13%	0.5%	11%
Munich/aromatic	0	4%	2%	31%
Cara, crystal	0	4%	1%	24%
Wheat	0	7%	1%	10%
Sugar	4%	22%	12%	100%
Honey	0%	8%	0.5%	7%
Spices	-	-	-	10%

TRIPEL

Double and triple (or two or three marks on a keg) once indicated a beer of higher gravity, and by the sixteenth century variations on the word "double" made their way into the names of beer styles. However, almost from the moment that Hendrik Verlinden of Witkap and the monks at Westmalle began selling their tripels, tripel meant pale and strong. As Lyle Brown noted before, spiciness sets tripels apart. "The spiciness must come from both hops and yeast and fermentation temperature. It can be subtle or strong, but it must be evident," he said.

Despite Westmalle's influence, a tripel need not be 9.6% abv and nearly 40 IBU. For instance, consider where moving from one similar beer to another takes us. British beer writer Roger Protz claims that Chimay created its *White (Cinq Cents)* in reaction to the popularity of *Orval*. In turn, while we've noted that *Orval* should fairly be called a style unto itself, it features saison characteristics. The point being, we might consider *Moinette Blonde* in tripel-ish terms. *Moinette* hails from notable saison producer Brasserie Dupont, and has been described as a "super saison." Starting at 1.066 (16.5 °P), but attenuating in typical Dupont character beyond 90%, *Moinette* packs in more than 8% alcohol—flashing all the fruit, spice, and alcohol character expected in a tripel, although with a rustic quality resulting from the Dupont yeast and water high in bicarbonate.

In the case of tripels, the spiciness also may come from spice. Brouwerij Bosteels produces its popular and award-winning *Tripel Karmeliet*, for example, by using unspecified but noticeable spices and hopping at about half the rate of Westmalle. Bosteels also uses a much more complex grain bill, with unmalted and malted barley, oats, and wheat (six malts). In 2002 AleSmith Brewing in San Diego created a cult favorite in *Stumblin' Monk*, brewing it just one time but using three secret spices as well as coriander and orange peel. Although the alcohol (9.7% abv) was evident, *Stumblin' Monk* finished surprisingly dry.

This style invites experimentation of a different sort than that involved in building recipes for darker beers (the next two categories). *La Rulles Tripel*, from Brasserie deRulles in the Ardennes, is fermented from yeast acquired from *Orval*, bittered with high alpha American Warrior hops, and flavored with American Amarillo, the latter adding a mango accent to the distinctly honeyish tone set by the malt bill. The *De Ranke* brewery dry-hops *Guldenberg*.

Despite the range of grains in *Tripel Karmeliet*, most brewers will be better off with mostly Pilsener malts—supplemented with a very small amount of Munich or a bit of lighter colored caramel—and experimenting with spices, hopping, or fermentation regimen. For instance, in *Bink Tripel*, the mixture of Challenger and East Kent Goldings for bittering topped with spiciness from Saaz accents the earthy yeast quality evident in all the beers from Brouwerij Kerkom.

Tripels are the hoppiest, hoppiest being a relative term, of the Trappist-inspired beers, with BU:GU ratios reaching up to 1:2. However, many commercial versions, such as *Grimbergen Tripel* and *Gouden Carolus* from Het Anker, may be as low as 1:4 or 1:5.

Examples featured in this book: *Westmalle Tripel, Bink Tripel, Tripel Karmeliet, St Feuillien Tripel, Bishops Tippel Trippel, Victory Golden Monkey*

The recipe

The recipe for this beer, called *Epiphany Tripel*, includes honey because homebrewer Joel Plutchak started to brew before he realized he was low on sugar. That didn't keep the beer from winning Best of Show at the 1998 Brewers on the Bluff Brewer's

Dream competition in suburban Chicago, and as the prize, it was subsequently brewed at Mickey Finn's Brewing Company in Libertyville, Illinois.

"Mickey Finn's version was smoother," Plutchak said. "Where mine had a few rough edges—a touch of fusel alcohol, a bit of graininess, a little too much sweetness for style—theirs was beguilingly drinkable. I credit their better temperature control in the mash and fermentation for much of the difference. The story goes that patrons found the beer so drinkable that the

Epiphany Tripel

Original Gravity: 1.087 (20.9 °P)

Final Gravity: 1.021 (5.3 °P)

Alcohol by Volume: 8.6%

IBU: 24

Grist Bill:

Pilsener malt 86.2%

Aromatic malt 1.7%

Wheat malt 1.7%

Table sugar 6.9%

Honey 3.4%

Hops:

Tettnang (4.5% AA), 60 minutes (23 IBU)

Saaz (3.5% AA), 5 minutes (1 IBU)

Mash: 151-152° F (66-67° C)

Boil: 75 minutes

Yeast: Wyeast 3787

Fermentation: 65-70° F (18-21° C)

Table 11.8 Dubbel Style Guidelines, Commercial Examples

	Original Gravity SG (°Plato)	Alcohol (abv)	Apparent Extract (FG)	Color SRM (EBC)	Bitterness IBU
BJCP	1.062-1.075 (15.2-18.2 °P)	6-7.5%	1.010-1.018 (2.6-4.6 °P)	10-14 (20-28)	25-38
Brewers Association	1.050-1.070 (12.5-17 °P)	6-7.5%	1.012-1.016 (3-4 °P)	14-18 (28-36)	18-25
Westmalle Dubbel	1.064 (15.6 °P)	7.3%	1.008 (2.1 °P)	37 (74)	24
Grimbergen Dubbel	1.059 (14.5 °P)	6.4%	1.011 (2.8 °P)	15.5 (31)	18
New Belgium Abbey	1.063 (15.5 °P)	7%	1.011 (2.8 °P)	27.5 (55)	24

Color measured in EBC, converted to SRM by dividing by 1.97 (see page 18).

alcohol would hit them unawares. It was released in the beginning of March, but they took it off the menu for the busy St. Patrick's Day crowd, so nobody would get injured.

"The recipe itself is based on advice I got from California homebrewer Scott Kaczorowski. I have since played around with adding flaked maize, and using British Pilsener malt, but (this) recipe is still my favorite. Early on I used white candi sugar (rocks) but decided it didn't make a difference. I've also used some other yeasts, but the 3787 is what I like best for tripels; not much banana, nice phenolics."

Table 11.9 Characteristics
for Homebrewed Dubbels

	Low	High	Average
SG	1.069 (16.8 °P)	1.088 (21.5 °P)	1.075
abv	6.4%	8.9%	7.7%
Apparent Attenuation	69%	86%	78%
IBU	14	30	24
BU:GU	0.25	0.50	0.32
SRM	11	20	7

Table 11.10 Grain Bills
for Homebrewed Dubbels

	Low	High	Average	Incidence
Pilsener/pale	60%	92%	61%	100%
Munich/aromatic	0	40%	8%	52%
Cara/crystal up 60 °L	0	40%	2%	73%
Roasted/chocolate	0	18%	3%	58%
Special "B"	0	12%	5%	88%
Wheat	0	22%	1%	21%
Sugar	3%	18%	10%	100%
Spices	-	-	-	12%

DUBBEL

Because they are dark and strong but not too strong, dubbels drink most like Trappist ales of the past, and to many they represent the "abbey" style. *Dubbels* introduced many drinkers to Belgian beer, in part because of *Chimay Red* and in part because so many brewpubs occasionally brew a dubbel.

Although Belgian brewers favor Pilsener for the base malt and lean heavily on dark caramel syrup for color and complexity, Americans lean toward pale ale malt as well as Pilsener in the base and a much wider range of specialty malts. Among homebrewers, Special "B" appears in almost nine out of ten recipes, often along with CaraMunich.

The range of fermentables varies little from dark strong. In fact, like the line between golden strong ale and tripel, the one between dubbel and dark strong gets blurred. Where does a beer like *Maredsous 8* (1.069, but stronger than 8% abv) fit?

Gordon Strong, who wrote the guidelines, explains that much of the distinction is a matter of intensity. "The main differences are apparently rooted in the alcohol strength," he said. "Dark strongs are a broader style with a greater range of commercial interpretations, but they all have a complex balance of interesting flavors and aromas with a malty flavor and a darker-than-pale color. Dark strongs have a greater alcohol component, but have more malt and yeast character to match. The balance remains similar, but the intensity of perceptual characteristics is proportionally greater in Belgian dark strongs."

Examples featured in this book: *Westmalle Dubbel, New Belgium Abbey, Ommegang, Flying Fish Dubbel, Chimay Red, Maredsous 8*

The recipe

The first Belgian-style beer Tomme Arthur brewed after he went to work at Pizza Port was *Dubbel Overhead Abbey*, and he figures that of the many Belgian-inspired beers he brews, it is the closest "to style." He bases this dubbel recipe on his own for Pizza Port.

"The depth of a great abbey beer lies in a malt sweetness, combined with an alcoholic warmth and a yeast finish," he said. "All of these make a rounded product that can be consumed in greater quantities. The key to a great beer, no matter the style, is the role yeast plays in the development of flavors— in lager beer, smooth crisp flavors; in Belgian styles, a wider palate of flavors but homogenized so no one completely dominates the beer."

The malt bill plays on that. "(It) is very complex and has specific requirements and components," Arthur said. "When I think of these beers, I think of rich, toasted, caramel with a fruity essence, and rocky head. These beers are magical in their complexity. My personal preference is to brew this type of beer without the use of chocolate, as I find it more often than not is used at too high a level. Most dubbels are rich in both aroma and flavor. ... This complex grain bill with many aromatic malts ensures a killer aroma and satisfying beer."

Arthur holds dark candi sugar to 6% of fermentables in *Dubbel Overhead*, and thinks that if it gets higher than 8%, it can take away from the malt complexity. He calls the raisins a "secret ingredient" and uses them in *Dubble Overhead* as well as other beers.

Tomme Arthur's Dubbel

Original Gravity: 1.067 (16.4 °P)

Final Gravity: 1.014 (3.6 °P)

Alcohol by Volume: 6.9%

IBU: 15

Grist Bill:

Belgian Pilsener malt 58.8%

Wheat malt 8.4%

Belgian aromatic malt 6.7%
Belgian or German Munich malt 4.2%

CaraMunich 3.4%

Gambrinus Honey malt (substitute-CaraVienna) 3.4%

Belgian Special "B" 3.4%

Belgian biscuit 3.4%

Dark candi sugar (rocks) 8.4%

Raisins (end of boil)—comparable to 4 ounces for a 5-gallon batch (113 grams for 19 liters)

Hops:

Styrian Goldings, 90 minutes (11 IBU)

Liberty, 60 minutes (4 IBU)

Mash: 152° F (67° C)

Boil: 90 minutes

Yeast: White Labs WLP500

Fermentation: Start at 64° F (18° C), 5-7 days

Secondary: Cold condition for 2 weeks

Table 11.11 Dark Strong Style Guidelines, Commercial Examples

	Original Gravity SG (°Plato)	Alcohol (abv)	Apparent Extract (FG)	Color SRM (EBC)	Bitterness IBU
BJCP	1.075-1.110+ (18.2-26 °P)	8-12+%	1.010-1.024 (2.6-6 °P)	15-20 (30-40)	15-25+
Brewers Association	1.064-1.096 (16-23 °P)	7-11%	1.012-1.024 (3-6 °P)	7-20 (14-40)	20-50
Rochefort 10	1.096 (23 °P)	11.3%	1.011 (2.8 °P)	45 (90)	27
Westvleteren 12	1.090 (21.5 °P)	10.2%	1.012 (3.1 °P)	40 (79)	38
St. Bernardus 12	1.090 (21.5 °P)	10%	1.014 (3.6 °P)	43 (86)	22

Color measured in EBC, converted to SRM by dividing by 1.97 (see page 18).

Table 11.12 Characteristics for Homebrewed Dark Strong Ales

	Low	High	Average
SG	1.070 (17.1 °P)	1.112 (26.3 °P)	1.098
abv	8%	13.1%	9.8%
Apparent Attenuation	70%	84%	75%
IBU	24	52	33
BU:GU	0.22	0.46	0.33
SRM	9	28	16

Table 11.13 Grain Bills
for Homebrewed Dark Strong Ales

	Low	High	Average	Incidence
Pilsener/pale	50%	85%	64%	100%
Munich/aromatic	0	38%	12%	68%
Cara/crystal up 60 °L	0	22%	6%	71%
Roasted/chocolate	0	12%	2%	32%
Special "B"	0	9%	4%	89%
Wheat	0	25%	1%	25%
Sugar	0	19%	11%	96%
Spices	-	-	-	12%

DARK STRONG ALE

Recipes for the best Belgian examples of beers strong and dark use relatively simple grain bills to create astonishingly complex beers. Westvleteren includes only Pilsener and pale malts, plus various sugars. *St. Bernardus 12* contains Pilsener malt, one "black" malt for aging stability, plus light and dark sugars. *Rochefort 10* uses two malts (Pilsener and a caramel), then light and dark sugar. On the other hand, the average homebrew recipe in our sample group contains 5.4 malts, plus sugar. A Belgian brewer might not approve. "I tell people, "You are in the kitchen," " said Marc Limet of Brouwerij Kerkom. "When you put too much dark malt in, it is the same as spices or hops. Too much is too much."

Dark strong ales challenge a brewer on two levels: formulating a recipe for complexity without creating a phenolic soup, and managing fermentation for the strongest of the Trappist-inspired ales.

For the first, it helps to remember the basic advice that you want to develop flavor with the lightest-colored malts possible, creating complexity by building in layers. Think of the flavors that you'll get not only from malts, but also whatever you use for a dark sugar contribution and also from fermentation.

Fermentation concerns begin with yeast selection. After a longer primary than Westvleteren, for instance, Rochefort finishes secondary in about three days. The Westmalle yeast that Westvleteren uses would still be brimming with banana and clove character after three days, but Rochefort's yeast doesn't generate the same esters.

Management starts with pitching the proper amount of yeast. Because worts with higher starting gravities already lead to increased acetate esters, the importance of beginning fermentation at a lower temperature—perhaps in an open, flatter environment such as at Westvleteren—increases. Although fermentation may get fast and furious, and temperatures alarmingly high, be sure to give the yeast time to attenuate fully.

Hops play a peripheral role in strong darks, with no or little aroma. The BU:GU ratio often is 1:3 or even 1:4.

Examples featured in this book: *Rochefort 10, Achel Bruin Extra, Westvleteren 8, St. Bernardus 12, Emperor of the Grand Cru, Southampton Abbot 12*

The recipe

Noel Blake brewed this beer on Super Bowl Sunday in 2001, and it took second place in the National Homebrew Competition. He was inspired by tasting notes from the first time he tried *Westvleteren 12*, and shortly thereafter used those notes again to write a description of his "dream beer" for a national contest:

"My dream beer is a strong Belgian ale with a burnished cherrywood color that pours with a fine, long lasting mousse. I allow her to rest in the widemouthed goblet for several minutes, observing the upward procession of fine bubbles and the incredible stability of her stiff, meringuelike head. Upon raising the glass to my nose, a tremendous burst of dried apricots comes in several waves as if exhaled by angels. Underneath, a steady pulse of cedar, leather, and black figs lets me know that she is indeed possessed of an extraordinary animus. Each sip sends tendrils of pear, prune, and raisin flavors to the four corners of my palate. And oh yes, there is the considerable alcohol that dwells within, not without effect, yet reticent to declare itself. Her body is unctuous, creamy, and finely balanced. The inevitable result is that this beer must eventually be swallowed, and so each sip is dispatched to its final resting place with a flourish of bracing bitterness and a summary dry finish. I could savor her for hours, but alas, the drams are far too few.

"Food pairings: A rich plate of cheeses would pair well with my first glass of this beer: aromatic Gorgonzola, fruity *Pont l'Eveque*, creamy Saint Andre, and tangy *Idiazabal*. A French-style fruit tarte, with a buttery crust, custard, apricots ringed with blueberries, and a brilliant glaze over all would be a heavenly pairing with my second glass. To finish the session, my third glass would be served with my grandfather's favorite dessert: fresh figs, and cream."

Because Blake won the essay contest, Brewery Ommegang set out to create a beer that matched the description, brewing a single batch and bottling some for him. Ommegang's Randy Thiel remembers working on the test batches in 2001. "It seemed we were missing the complexity you get in beers like Westvleteren

Noel Blake's Three Philosophers Ale

Original Gravity: 1.087 (20.9 °P)

Final Gravity: 1.020 (5.1 °P)

Alcohol by Volume: 8.8%

IBU: 30-35

Grist Bill:

Belgian pale malt 62%

Belgian Munich malt 16%

Flaked wheat malt 6%

Special "B" 4%

CaraMunich 3%

CaraVienna 2%

Sucrose 7%

Hops:

Northern Brewer (7.5 AA) for 75 minutes (30-35 IBU)

Mash: 154° F (68° C)

Boil: 75 minutes

Yeast: Wyeast 3787

Fermentation: 65-70° F (18-21° C), 3 days

Secondary: 67° F (19° C), 3 weeks

Tertiary: 67° F (19° C), 2 weeks

Process notes: The Special "B," CaraMunich, and CaraVienna were steeped at the end of the mash and through lautering

Fermentation notes: Wort was pitched at 68° F (20° C) on top of an existing oxygenated slurry. A wet towel was placed on the outside of the carboy, and within six hours the krausen was nearing the neck of the carboy, from which it would emerge from time to time over the next couple of days. Sucrose syrup was added after primary fermentation. After three weeks, racked again at 1.025 and allowed to finish for two more weeks. Bottled with dextrose and a fresh tube of 3787

and Rochefort," he said. "The trial batches were missing the depth of character, the esters. They were two dimensional."

During a tasting session, Don Feinberg finally said, "It needs more fruitiness," picked up a bottle of *Boon Kriek* and dumped it into the dark ale. It became part of the recipe. Brewery Ommegang made the beer a regular offering in 2003, adding *Lindemans Kriek* to the base "quad" style.

Why *Three Philosophers*? The name of the beer comes from an unpublished manuscript by William Blake called *An Island in the Moon*. It opens with the following paragraph:

"In the Moon, is a certain Island near by a mighty continent, which small island seems to have some affinity to England. & what is more extraordinary, the people are so much alike & their language so much the same that you would think you was among your friends. In this Island dwells three Philosophers: Suction the Epicurean, Quid the Cynic, and Sipsop the Pythagorean."

Hence, *Three Philosophers*.

Noel Blake's tasting notes state that compared to *Westvleteren 8*, his homebrewed beer lacked the rich, creamy mouthfeel and abundant head, and leaned more towards dark fruit than apricot notes.

BEERS WITHOUT HOMES

Tomme Arthur of Pizza Port brews many "beers that don't have homes," those that don't quite fit into a style category. Were he a homebrewer, that wouldn't be a problem. Welcome to BJCP Category 16E, Belgian Specialty Ale. As noted in the category description: "This is a catch-all category for any Belgian-style beer not fitting any other Belgian style category. The category can be used for clones of specific beers, to produce a beer fitting a broader style that doesn't have its own category … or to create an artisanal or experimental beer of the brewer's own choosing. Creativity is the only limit in brewing, but the entrant must identify what is special about their entry."

Since BJCP guidelines also allow for other experimental beers, this is the category where you might enter a beer in the spirit of the growing number of Belgian spinoffs created by American craftbrewers. Brewing these gives you a chance to haul out the picture of the Victor Horta staircase and remember the words of Peter Bouckaert of New Belgium Brewing: "This is inspiring. When you think of Belgian beer, that's what we are trying to do, trying to create a piece of beauty."

Of course, you could do that for any of the previous styles as well.

Examples featured in this book: *Orval, Temptation, Nostradamus*

The recipe

Dan Morey makes no bones about creativity. He set out to re-create *Orval*. This recipe for *laVal Abbey Special* won Best of Show at the Ninth Annual Dayton Beerfest, and later third place Best of Show at the BABBLE Brew-Off 2005 in suburban Chicago. Although Morey is devoted to Belgian styles—a few years ago he put together a twelve-page paper on "Designing Great Belgian Ales" for his homebrew club—this was his first pass at *Orval*.

"The first time I had this beer (in college), I loved it. Wow, the hops and the *Brett*. Later, for work, I traveled to Lille, France, several times a year for a few years. Every day after work, I stopped in the hotel bar and had a nice goblet of fresh *Orval* before returning to my room. I always intended on trying to clone it (one of the few beers worthy of cloning, in my opinion), but I never got around to it. Then Bastogne (yeast from White Labs, WLP510) came out; well, that did it. I had to finally do it, and it was wonderful."

He looked at clone recipes, read descriptions, and built his recipe profile. "I broke each recipe down, looking at the percent of IBUs contributed by each addition. Taking the weighted averages, I found that 86% of the IBUs were added around 80 minutes from knockout, and the remaining 14% at 15 minutes from knockout. The average amount of dry hops came out to 1.6 ounces for 5 gallons (46 grams per 19 liters). I used Perle instead of Hallertau because of the higher AA and figured the flavor would not be discernible after 80 minutes. I did not have Styrian Goldings at the time, so I went with American-grown Goldings."

Did that make the difference, or was it simply adding the dregs of two bottles of *Orval* in secondary? "It was a no-brainer," Morey said. "Get the real thing, plus a couple of *Orvals* to enjoy at the same time. *Brett* is essential. At bottling the beer was rather boring, and the hops seemed subdued. The *Brett* is really aromatic and helped accentuate the hops. It took a not-so-interesting beer and made it special."

Judges obviously agreed. "The combination of bitterness and *Brett* is right on," one wrote. "Bitterness is low for this beer, and hop flavor is underdone, but the *Brett* comes through very well," wrote another.

Drinking the last of the batch, Morey made plans for the next one. "Overall, I'm pretty pleased with the beer. It is really close to the real thing," he said. "I think the grain-sugar bill is

laVal Abbey Special

Original Gravity: 1.057 (14 °P)

Final Gravity: 1.009 (2.3 °P) at bottling (1.006 after a year)

Alcohol by Volume: 6.3%

IBU: 32

Grist Bill:

  Moravian Pilsener malt 76%

  CaraVienna 13%

  Amber candi sugar 11%

Hops:

  Perle (7.7 % AA) for 80 minutes (28 IBU)

  Goldings (4.3% AA) for 15 minutes (4 IBU)

  Goldings (4.3% AA) dry hop, 1.6 ounces for 5 gallons

Mash: 154° F (68° C)

Boil: 90 minutes

Yeast: White Labs WLP510

  Dregs of 2 bottles of *Orval* added at bottling

Fermentation: 72° F (22° C), 13 days

Secondary: 72° F (22° C), 14 days, dry hops added for last week

right on, no changes there. However, the hops do need to be increased. Bitterness could be raised to about 35 IBUs instead of 32. It needs more hops in the flavor addition (15 minutes), and dry hops should be increased to about 2-2.5 ounces per 5 gallons (56-70 grams per 19 liters). Also, I would use Styrian Goldings for the late additions instead of American Goldings. I definitely would stick with dregs from *Orval* at bottling over a pure *Brettanomyces* culture. I really doubt *Orval* has a pure strain of *Brett* that they are using."

This beer also has a fine story behind the name. "I believe *Orval* is pronounce Or-Val. It is kind of like a question do you want this Or Val?" Morey said. "It just happens my wife's name is Val. So in honor of her I decided to call my beer 'the' Val (a statement). 'The' just doesn't have the right ring to it, so I went with 'la,' French feminine for 'the.' Visually, the name is symmetrical and has balance. It just looked good on a label."

Bibliography

Arthur, Tomme and Tom Nickel. "Don't Call It a Belgian ... ," *Zymurgy* 28, no. 2 (March-April 2005), 32-37.

Beaumont, Stephen. *Premium Beer Drinker's Guide*. Willowdale, Ontario: Firefly Books, 2000.

Casey, Gregory. "Origins and Controlling Esters and Higher Alcohols in Beer." Presentation at Rocky Mountain Microbrewing Symposium, Colorado Springs, Colo. 2005.

Corran, H.S. *A History of Brewing*. 1975. London: David & Charles, 1975.

Daniels, Ray. *Designing Great Beers*. Boulder, Colo.: Brewers Publications, 1996.

De Clerck, Jean. *A Textbook of Brewing*. London: Chapman & Hall, 1957.

DeBenedetti, Christian. "Inside Orval: Sanctity Meets Modern Times in an Evolving Classic." *Brewing Techniques* 6, no. 3 (May-June 1998). Available at *www.brewingtechniques.com/library/ backissues/ issue6.3/debenedetti.html*

Deglas, Christian and Guy Derdelinckx. *The Classic Beers of Belgium.* Ann Arbor, Mich.: G.W. Kent, 1997.

Dorsch, Jim. "Dubbel Vision." *Zymurgy* 23, no. 1 (January-February 2000), 32-35+.

Elsen, Casimir. "Abdij Notre-Dame de Scourmont te Chimay." *Den Bierproever* 55 (May 1999), 4-5.

Fix, George. "Belgian Malts: Some Practical Observations." *Brewing Techniques* 1, no. 1 (1993). Available at *www.brewingtechniques.com/library/backissues/issue1.1/fix.html*

Fix, George. *Principles of Brewing Science.* Boulder, Colo.: Brewers Publications, 1989.

Fix, George and Laurie. *An Analysis of Brewing Techniques.* Boulder, Colo.: Brewers Publications, 1997.

Frane, Jeff. "How Sweet It Is—Brewing With Sugar," *Zymurgy* 17, no. 1 (Spring 1994), 38-41.

Frane, Jeff. "The Link Between Heaven and Earth," *Brew Your Own* 2, no. 4 (April 1996), 23-26.

Gladwell, Malcolm. *Blink: The Power of Thinking Without Thinking*. New York: Little, Brown, 2005.

Grossman, Bob. "Brewing's Sweetest Secret." *Zymurgy* 25, no. 4 (July-August 2002), 36-39+.

Hall, Michael. "Brew By the Numbers—Add Up What's in Your Beer." *Zymurgy* 18, no. 2 (Summer 1995), 54-61.

Hornsey, Ian. *A History of Beer and Brewing.* Cambridge, England: Royal Society of Chemistry, 2003.

Jackson, Michael. *The Beer Hunter: The Burgundies of Belgium*. VHS. Bethesda, Md.: The Discovery Channel, 1989.

Jackson, Michael. *The Great Beers of Belgium*. 3rd ed. Philadelphia: Running Press, 1998.

Jackson, Michael. *The Great Beers of Belgium*. 4th ed. London: Prion Books, 2001.

Jackson, Michael. *Michael Jackson's Beer Companion*. Philadelphia: Running Press, 1993.

Jackson, Michael. *The New World Guide to Beer*. Philadelphia: Running Press, 1988.

Jackson, Michael. "The Rockies' Rival to Rodenbach." *The Beer Hunter*. Available at *www.beerhunter.com/documents/19133-001604.html*

Jackson, Michael. *World Guide to Beer.* London: Quarto, 1977.

Johnson, G. M. "A Belgian Mashing System Suitable for Light Beers." *Journal of the Institute of Brewing* (1916): 237-251.

Johnson, G. M. "Brewing in Belgium and Belgian Beers." *Journal of the Federated Institutes of Brewing* (1895): 450-470.

Line, Dave. *Brewing Beer Like Those You Buy.* Ann Arbor, Mich: G.W. Kent, 1978.

Lodahl, Martin. "Belgian Trappist and Abbey Beers," *Brewing Techniques* 2, no. 6 (November-December 1994). Available at *www.brewingtechniques.com/library/styles/2_6style.html*

Logsdon, Dave, Dave Bryant, and Larry Nielsen. "Wheat Beer Flavor From Thirteen Different Yeasts in Head-to-Head Competition." Presentation at the Craft Brewers Conference, New Orleans, 2003.

Magerman, Bob. "Trappist Beer From Rochefort." *Bier Passion* 11 (April/May 2001), 38-41+.

Markowski, Phil. *Farmhouse Ales: Culture and Craftsmanship in the Belgian Tradition.* Boulder, Colo.: Brewers Publications, 2004.

Miller, Thomas. "On the Yeast." *Brew Your Own* 6, no. 9 (November 2000), 46-48.

Mosher, Randy. *The Brewers's Companion*. Seattle: Alephenalia Publications, 1995.

Mosher, Randy. *Radical Brewing*. Boulder, Colo.: Brewers Publications, 2004.

Noonan, Greg. *New Brewing Lager Beer*. Boulder, Colo.: Brewers Publications, 1996.

Orval. *A Visit to the Orval Brewery*. DVD. Villers-devant-Orval: Ripley/Orval, 2002.

Palmer, John. "Sweetness: Brewing Sugars and How to Use Them." *Brew Your Own* 10, no. 2 (March-April 2004), 34-39.

Perrier-Robert, Annie, and Charles Fontaine. *Belgium by Beer, Beer by Belgium*. Luxembourg: Schortgen, Esch/Alzette, 1996.

Protz, Roger. *The Ale Trail*. Kent, England: Eric Dobby Publishing, 1995.

Protz, Roger. *Heavenly Beer*. London: Carroll & Brown Limited, 2002.

Rajotte, Pierre. *Belgian Ale*. Boulder, Colo.: Brewers Publications, 1992.

Strong, Gordon. "Designing Great Belgian Dark Strong Ales." Presentation at National Homebrewers Conference, Chicago, 2003.

Strong, Gordon. "Designing Great Dubbels." Presentation at Masters Championship of Amateur Brewing IV, Cleveland, 2002.

Unger, Richard. *Beer in the Middle Ages and Renaissance.* Philadelphia: University of Pennsylvania Press, 2004.

Urban, Dennis and Mark Staples. "Great Northern Brewers' Trippel Yeast Experiment." *Zymurgy* 24, no. 6 (November-December 2001), 50-52+.

Van den Steen, Jef. *Les Trappistes: Les Abbayes et Leurs Bières.* Brussels: Editions Racine, 2003.

Verheyden, Filip. "Trappist Beers from La Trappe." *Bier Passion* 5 (December/January/February 2001), 8-10.

Webb, Tim. *Good Beer Guide to Belgium & Holland.* St. Albans, England: CAMRA, 2002.

Webb, Tim. "The New Brewers of Belgium." *All About Beer Magazine* 20, no. 4 (September 1999), 24-27+.

Woods, John and Keith Rigley. *The Beers of Wallonia.* Wedmore, England: The Artisan Press, 1996.

Young, Gordon. "Free Market Monks in the 20th Century." *Beer the Magazine* 2, no. 3 (September 1994), 29-32+.

Index

Entries in **boldface** indicate photographs or captions.